Free Will and the Divine Nature of Humans

John S. Talbot

Jim & Bonny
out! Hope this doesn't freak you
it — most of the 3rd Chapter
in Betty's home. Her kindness
and helpfulness contributed a great
deal to this book.

Love John

ISBN 978-0-9787134-0-0

Library of Congress Control Number: 2007904225
Publisher: Creative Idea Communications LLC
Sarasota, Florida

A Creative Idea Communications Book,
P.O. Box 195
5317 Fruitville Rd.
Sarasota, FL 34232
urdivinefreewill.com

Cover design, layout, and some internal figures by Michael A. Lynch.
Cover photo by Alene C. Lynch

Table of Contents

Preface

"Are you kidding? You want to go into physics? You must be out of your mind." Not very encouraging words to hear from your high-school physics teacher who was the one that inspired you to become a physicist. The world of physics had sprung to life under the nurturing hand of this exceptional teacher. I had never had any trouble with mathematics, so when he taught us about the fascinating world of 20th-Century physics, my marks suddenly took off and I devoured the subject. Since I got straight A's in his class, I think he took this rather strange response to my announcement because he wanted to make sure I realized what a tough field I was planning to enter.

The truth was that I had always wanted to go into science, but I didn't know what field. My father's field of chemistry with its smelly potions and loud-bang possibilities wasn't for me. On the other hand, cutting up frogs and labeling different types of flora and fauna didn't thrill me either, so biology and botany were out. Math was great but you had to be obsessed with it in order to make any kind of living at it in the 1940's.

So despite my mentor's discouraging words, I decided to pursue physics when I got out of the Navy. I had to apply to six different colleges and universities because most of them were overcrowded due to the huge influx of veterans eager to take advantage of the GI Bill. I was accepted at three, two of which I felt were the best prospects: Rutgers, an all-male, technically oriented university, and Hobart, a small liberal-arts co-ed college in upper New York State. Even though Rutgers was the obvious choice for a physics undergraduate, I chose the liberal-arts school not only to get a broader education, but because those lovely creatures called women went there—I'd had about all of the all-male scene I could handle after the Navy. It was an amazingly lucky choice. Not only did I meet my life-long soul mate, but I also got probably one of the best educations in Western Civilization's philosophy and history one could hope to get in one lifetime. As for the physics and math departments, what they lacked in equipment and staff they made up for in small intimate classes and surprisingly competent professors. With that background I easily got a job after graduation as a research physicist at Westinghouse Research Labs in Pittsburgh, PA.

When I got that job at Westinghouse for the astounding sum of $396 a month, it was partly because of a naïve mistake I made when I applied for it. I wrote directly to the man whose name was in the recruiting brochure. It turned out that he was the head of Personnel for *all* of the

Westinghouse companies. Why he agreed to see me personally, I'll never know, but it was obvious even to a wet-behind-the-ears kid like me that he hadn't done an interview in years. Fortunately, I was smart enough to volunteer as little information as possible while answering all his fumbling questions as pleasantly and succinctly as I could. It was a slam dunk. Nice man that he was, he offered me a job on the spot.

My next successful interview after the three-month orientation program was with Dr. Max Garbuny, a physicist in the Westinghouse Research Lab. Max was a brilliant and delightfully crazy man who would bid slam on a mediocre Bridge hand at the drop of a hat. The disgusting part was that more often than not, he would make it. Max was a German Jew who fled Germany after attending a Nazi rally in Nuremberg. He said he became convinced of the extreme danger he was in when he found himself almost wanting to raise his arm in the Nazi salute during Hitler's speech even though he was fully aware of the Nazis' murderous hatred of the Jews. It was obvious that the man's mesmerizing power was going to hypnotize even the decent German citizens into conducting devastating pogroms against the Jews. Being the intelligent man that he was, he knew that flight was his only logical option. It was my very good fortune that it was, because under his tutelage, I became a fairly competent physicist.

Westinghouse had a policy of awarding anyone $50 for a disclosure of an invention and $75 if the company decided to go ahead and apply for a formal patent. Naturally, everyone at the labs submitted disclosures on everything in sight. For example, one of our more gifted scientists submitted a patent for an ingenious detection device that could intercept radiation, measure the angle of incidence, and time the event without requiring batteries. It was only after they accepted his disclosure that he revealed to them that they had just awarded him $50 for inventing the sun dial. It was his way of telling them that they shouldn't have rejected one of his previous disclosures because he knew more science than they did!

Even though my wife and I thought we'd never be able to spend all of our generous salary each month, we quickly discovered a talent for doing just that. It was inevitable that I would be quick to join the patenting parade to get those extra bucks. Eventually, in addition to a number of other patents, I submitted a secret device with Max that won the very first "Most Meritorious Reward" at Westinghouse. With the $200 we each got from the special award, Dottie and I bought our first brand-new piece of furniture.

So there I was in a research lab, happily engaged in a profession I had spent so much time and hard work to achieve—and then my mother died. She was a very dear person to me and my family, and for that matter to everyone who got to know her. In fact, my wife says she agreed to marry me partly because she wanted my mother to be her mother-in-law. Mom's death from cancer was devastating to all of us.

Mom had been a very religious person in an inauspicious way and had passed her religious beliefs on to my sister and me. But when she died, I was faced with a dilemma. Where had she gone? There was no doubt in my mind that she would make heaven a better place just by her presence, but I was quite aware that she was very human and had all the minor foibles that we are all heir to. Where was the cruel dividing line in the vast moral territory between Reichsführer-SS Heinrich Himmler and Mother Teresa? What was the criteria for deciding who went to the Heaven side of that line and who went to Hell? Presumably, there had to be a point on the moral "goodness" scale where a tiny bit more would send someone to Heaven and a tiny bit less would send the poor soul to eternal damnation. Using belief that Jesus was the Son of God as an on-off switch to decide one's fate didn't make sense to me either if you considered all the wonderful people over the ages who'd never even heard of him. It's no wonder that the Roman Catholics invented Purgatory.

While fussing over this Judeo/Christian concept of Heaven and Hell, the Eastern idea of reincarnation started to look intriguing. Now that was something that I could relate to. Coming back again and again until we get it right might seem like a bit of a bore to many, but to me it made more sense than playing Russian Roulette with a seemingly arbitrary religious criteria. And even though reincarnation was not a tenet of the Christian belief and wasn't mentioned in the Bible, there was nothing that said that it couldn't be compatible with either one. So the idea of continuing my education by going to seminary and learning all I could about my own religion before continuing on to other religions started to appeal strongly. Seminary was just an application away and a few hundred heated "discussions" with my wife. Eventually, we reconciled our differences and off to seminary we went.

While in seminary I realized that although I was doing well in my religious studies, my forte was science. So instead of becoming a professor of comparative religions, why not teach science and math as an ordained minister, demonstrating that science and religion need not be incompatible? That required at least a Masters degree in science, so after graduating from seminary, I entered a post-graduate course in math and science at Columbia University while earning an income by serving as a curate at a little church on Park Avenue and a chaplain at the Ewing Cancer Hospital. It was while serving in the latter capacity that I started having very serious doubts about my calling to the priesthood..

I'd actually had some doubts in seminary, but as the Dean of the seminary told me, many seminarians go through periods of doubt. Since I was doing so well in my studies, he suggested that I finish my Masters of Sacred Theology and simply refuse ordination if my doubts had not been resolved. Good advice except for one thing: I was so busy attending class, studying for my canonicals, and writing weekly theses that I didn't really take the time to concentrate on the theological concepts that had started to make me a little uneasy. In fact it became easier and easier to let them slip into the background and just continue on the path that inevitably led to ordination.

And so along with a dozen other ordinands I was ordained as an Episcopal priest in the Cathedral of St. John the Divine in Manhattan as the state trumpets sounded triumphantly at the back of the quarter-mile long narthex. Can't get much more ordained than that. However, my position as priest became untenable when I began to minister to the cancer patients at Ewing. In the '50s these people almost without exception were dying. How could I comfort them with my religion if I wondered if I believed in it myself?

My fundamental problem was that I gradually realized that I didn't really think that Jesus Christ was God. Oddly enough, at the time I was ordained, there were a number of my fellow priests who didn't believe he was God, either, but felt that they could still stay in the priesthood as spiritual leaders. My position was that you shouldn't stay in a club as one of the leaders if you didn't believe in the club's rules. Obviously, there are and were some prominent ecclesiastical leaders like Bishop Spong and the late Bishop Pike, former Dean of St. John's Cathedral, who felt otherwise.

Once I quit the priesthood, my sole goal was to provide my family with a comfortable living as quickly as possible. Since there were no local jobs available in physics during the minor recession of the time, I took one as a technical writer and eventually as an advertising manager at an aerospace company. From that time on my rather eclectic career included owner of a one-man technical advertising agency, actor on the dinner-theater circuit, computer programmer, and teacher of an ESP-development course called Silva Mind Control, a course that changed the way I looked at reality.

I had read newspaper accounts about Silva and had read the book by Jose Silva, the man who invented the technique. He claimed that he could teach anyone to use extra-sensory perception to "see" a sick person at a distance and describe their illness without knowing them.

This was enough for me. Although the cost of the course was not insignificant for me in the late 70's, I felt it was worth it if it could actually teach me to describe the illness of someone I had never met. As far as I knew, no other course had ever claimed that it could teach you to do something like that. However, it was one thing to admit that I might be able to do it, and it was quite another to actually experience it.

I knew pretty much what to expect since I had read Silva's book before taking the class. The book is not very well written, unfortunately, and although it claims that you can learn the technique just by reading it, I knew that for me at least I had to take the course if I wanted to do something more than just feel good about myself. My only interest in the Silva Method was to experience real, provable, extra-sensory perception.

It worked. In fact it worked so well that I eventually wound up teaching the course myself.

Although I taught hundreds of people, I never got over the amazement of seeing these ordinary people develop their ability to identify the illness—and often even the appearance and personality—of people they didn't know who lived far away. The irony of the situation did not escape me. Here I was, a man trained in the hard-nosed field of physics, teaching an eclectic group of people made up of housewives, business men, hippies, bikers, children, and the occasional drunk how to develop a talent unrecognized by science! What in the world was going on here?

In addition to Silva, something had happened to me in my childhood that compounded the problem. Not too many years before I started teaching Silva, there had been accounts of some people who had been clinically dead and then revived who seemed to have had an extraordinary experience. They spoke of rising out of their bodies, hearing a strange buzzing sound, passing through a dark tunnel with the aid of long lost relatives and friends, seeing an incredibly brilliant light emanating from a loving being, and going through a life review with him before being persuaded or deciding to return to the living.

Raymond A. Moody, Jr., M.D. wrote a book about this experience called *Life After Life*. When I first read Moody's book in the 70's I was stunned. This was what had happened to me when I was eight or nine years old. The only problem was that it wasn't exactly the same since I didn't remember any blinding light emanating from the man I had spoken to nor any formal life review.

It all happened when I had a tonsillectomy. I had had a lot of colds when I was a kid, and it was the wisdom of the day in the 1930's that tonsillitis was the most likely cause. Therefore, the cure was to take out those pesky organs that weren't of any use to anyone. Although no one ever said that I died while I was under the ether (a very tricky anesthetic), later when I was in a Navy sick bay in 1946 on an aircraft carrier docked in Norfolk, Virginia, a Navy doctor, a Commander on the base, discovered that my surgeon had really botched my tonsillectomy operation. The Commander even had a number of Navy doctors come in to take a look at what a mess my childhood doctor had made of my tonsils. It made me wonder if some sort of anomaly had occurred during that long-ago operation—why else would a presumably experienced pediatrician surgeon, who had supposedly performed hundreds of tonsillectomies, have done such a poor job on a simple procedure?

When I read about the near-death experiences of the people in Moody's book, I realized they were almost identical with what I had experienced when I was undergoing the operation. First I noticed a rather unpleasant grating sound. Then I was surrounded by a bunch of people who were telling me not to be afraid and that they would take good care of me. I eventually met a wonderful man who inspired in me a profound love.

Although my impression is that the man and I talked about a great many things that I have since forgotten, I remember that he somehow revealed to me that "that mean Leroy kid" who threw sand on me at the beach was perhaps more to be pitied than censored.. He also said that I shouldn't be contemptuous of people if they didn't understand things which I thought were obvious. I was rather shocked that he would suggest such a thing since I was experiencing that same kind of contempt from my father and some of the teachers at school. I assured him that I would *never* treat other people that way. I must confess that I may have slipped a bit on that score over the years.

He also insisted that I had to go back because I had to do something, but he wouldn't tell me what it was. "You'll have to discover what it is all by yourself," he said. When I protested that I didn't want to leave, he pointed out how devastated my mother would be if I didn't, something I couldn't bring myself to contemplate. So I reluctantly agreed. Just before I started back, he admonished me not to tell my parents what had happened because they wouldn't understand.

The trip back was horrible with all the people I had met when I first came into this place circling around me and telling me that I had to go back. Again the grating sound occurred just before I woke up from the ether in the recovery room.

It wasn't until I was back home in our apartment that I decided to ask my mom and dad who all the people were who were with me in the operating room. I thought if I asked that way, even though I knew that they weren't really in the operating room but in that special place that I went to, then they might be able to tell me what had happened to me. After all, if they recognized this as an experience that had happened to other people before, maybe they wouldn't get upset like the man said they would if I told them what had actually happened. Needless to say, they had no idea what I was talking about.

Over the days and weeks that followed I gradually revealed more and more of what I thought had happened during the operation. My father adamantly insisted that it was all just a dream, but even though I thought my dad was the font of all information about everything, I couldn't forget about it but just tucked it away as a fascinating but inexplicable experience.

However, many years later I read an article that claimed that people recorded everything that people around them said when they were supposedly totally unconscious. I told my dad that perhaps this was what I had experienced when I was under the ether, but surprisingly, he disagreed. He said that that didn't explain all the things I reported had happened to me during my experience. I was dumfounded to realize that my father no longer thought it was just a dream. Over the years, he had apparently thought about the experience a great deal and had come to the conclusion that something extraordinary had really happened to me during that long-ago operation.

By the time I read Moody's book decades later, I couldn't talk to my dad about it since he had already passed away. So on a recent trip when my wife and I stopped off to see my sister, I asked her if she remembered any of this back when she was eleven or twelve. She said, "Oh good Lord, yes. You drove us all crazy with your insistence that there were a bunch of people with you during the operation."

For me the question of whether I died on the operating table and then came back doesn't really matter—the experience was so real that afterwards I was always trying to figure out what I was supposed to do that was so important that I had to come back. I remember that in my childish imagination I thought maybe I would be the one to invent an antigravity machine so that people could fly around like Buck Rogers and Flash Gordon!

So far, no luck.

I still don't know what the important task was that I was supposed to complete or accomplish. However, when I retired, it occurred to me that my long and varied career had put me in a unique position to take an informed look at the recent developments in science and religion. Perhaps I could come up with a point of view that could put a different slant on our understanding of this very strange life of ours.

The book you are about to read is what I think reality is all about. A Jewish friend of mine defined the Yiddish word, *chutzpah*, as a flea crawling up an elephant's leg, dead set on rape. In this endeavor of mine I may be providing a new definition for that wonderfully descriptive word. All I can guarantee is that it's as close to the truth and as honest an evaluation as I can give you. I hope you find in it at least an interesting speculation on why we are here in this very strange place we call the universe.

Introduction and Synopsis

We all act as if we have free will. You wouldn't be reading these lines if you didn't. Oh you might claim that all our actions are predetermined, but you don't act that way. Why bother with making any decisions to do anything if you're just a puppet on a string?

But if we have free will, then we must be something more than just our physical bodies because it implies that our actions are not always controlled by the deterministic laws of nature. We think that the part of us that is called "I" can determine what we do and say. Determinists say that there's no way that we can prove scientifically that that's the case, but let's just assume that we really do have free will and see what happens. For example, let's ask a seemingly silly question: Can accidents happen?

Surprisingly, both the scientific and the religious communities have argued over this question for centuries. The bottom line is this: if any accidents can happen then free will is possible. If they can't—if everything is predetermined either by God or by the natural laws of nature—then classical science says that every move of every subatomic particle and every thought of every living being is predetermined. Free will goes out the window.

In the physical world of the classical scientists, accidents never happen. It's been said that an asteroid or comet *accidentally* slammed into the world about 65 million years ago and wiped out the dinosaurs, allowing the small mammals to survive and evolve into us. That probably happened but it was no accident. Once that asteroid was formed billions of years ago it was predestined by natural laws to follow the path it took to hit the earth at that particular time regardless of the number of collisions it experienced in the interim. It didn't hit the Earth by accident.

But here we've been talking about *inanimate* objects. As soon as life enters the picture, classical scientists can't be as certain about determinism. The natural laws of nature don't seem to apply since no one has ever been able to predict the actions of any individual beyond the simplest basic reactions. For example, if you set a plate of delicious food in front of a starving man, you can predict with 99% probability that he will eat—unless, of course, he's Mahatma Gandhi on a hunger strike. And therein lies the problem of trying to predict what a human will do with absolute certainty.

One of the things that the classical scientists did feel secure about was that the universe was both infinite and eternal. And of course, if you had an infinite and eternal universe, who needed an infinite and eternal God? But in the 1920's the astronomer Edwin Hubble discovered that the "nebulae" that were thought to be gas clouds within our galaxy of the Milky

Way were actually very distant galaxies containing billions of stars. Furthermore, because the light from them was shifted to the red end of the light spectrum, he determined that they were flying away from us, just as they would if the universe started with a big explosion—that is, with a "Big Bang." The possibility of a creator God suddenly reentered the scientific picture of the universe.

Let's assume for the moment that there is a God. Now we have to question whether God knew everything that was going to happen as soon as He created the universe. This is indeed the position of some religious theologians because God is omniscient and therefore must know the future. However, most religious and spiritual institutions teach or at least imply that we have free will. We can choose whether we follow the path of Jesus, or Mohammed, or Buddha, or the prophets and rabbis and achieve salvation, heaven, nirvana, or what have you after we die. The choice is ours, otherwise no one would preach it. But if our destiny is already mapped out, it doesn't make a bit of difference what anybody exhorts us to do because all of our actions have been predetermined. So when the religious leaders encourage us to "follow Jesus," "tread the 8-fold paths of Buddha," or "be true to the Koran as written by the prophet Mohammed," they must believe that we have the free, God-given will to do so no matter what they claim they believe about predestination.

Therefore, we seem to have free will in a world in which every physical, inanimate, macroscopic object in this universe of ours is predetermined to move in predictable ways because of natural forces. The only conclusion you can draw from that is that if we admit that we have free will, then the success of classical science seems to prove that the part of us that exercises our free will can't be a part of this physical world. If that's the case, our brains didn't create our minds. But if our minds and our brains are two separate substances, how do they interact? After all, the brain is material and therefore subject to natural laws, while the mind is apparently capable of free will and can direct the brain to think outside the natural laws. How can this be?

Well, you may have noticed that up to now I have been using the terms "macroscopic" and "classical science" in this discussion. There's a good reason for that. Up until the 20th Century, science seemed to prove that everything was determined by cause and effect. At least that was true in what I've been calling the "macroscopic" world, or the world that is very much larger than the "microscopic" or subatomic world. Once we were able to examine the latter with modern detection techniques and derived new mathematical laws from the resulting data, scientists discovered that this classical point of view didn't apply. Individual subatomic particles like electrons, protons, neutrons, and all the other micro-particles were governed by laws of probability, not the deterministic laws of cause and effect.

One of the best known of these new mathematical laws is the Heisenberg uncertainty principle. It states that if you know exactly where a subatomic particle is, you can't know the direction it's traveling. And if you pin down the direction, you can't know where it is. This means that the best you can do is determine the percentage probability that it would be at a particular position and traveling in a particular direction.

Another new discovery that put classical scientists off their feed was that matter is both particle-like and wave-like at the same time! Consider light, itself. If light falls on a photographic film or a photoelectric surface, it acts like a particle. If it passes through a prism or a pair of parallel slits, it acts like a wave. An electron acts like a particle in a cathode-ray tube or a TV tube but like a wave when it passes through a crystal.

Then there was the nature of the atom, itself. Ernest Rutherford discovered in 1911 that atoms seemed to act like little planetary systems with electrons circling around a tiny positive nucleus. To get an idea of the sizes involved, if the nucleus were the size of a golf ball and placed in the center of a football stadium, the electrons would be less than the size of a gnat, circling it at the perimeter of the stadium. In other words, good old solid matter is mostly empty space!* You might well ask, "If that's true, then why don't we fall through to the center of the Earth?" We don't because the negative electrons on the surface of almost all physical matter form a repelling force. When we sit on a chair, we're actually floating a tiny distance above it on a field of energy. Things are getting really spooky.

But not quite as spooky as things got when Erwin Schrödinger invented a new quantum mechanics to explain all these phenomena mathematically. While the new science was hugely successful, it led to some really bizarre results. One of them was called the "Copenhagen Interpretation" which said in effect that if there are two or more possibilities of an event occurring, they only become real when they are observed! That means that our entire material world only becomes *determinate* when we observe it. Believe it or not this interpretation is accepted today by many in the modern scientific community because of the unprecedented success of quantum mechanics. Quantum physics has given us integrated circuits, the computer chip, laser technology, superconductivity, and many other modern wonders. It has also demonstrated with unprecedented substantiation that predetermination can no longer be accepted at the subatomic level.

So it would seem that this is the doorway to allow free will to enter the physical world. Our thoughts can influence the choices that are available to us and produce physical actions that are not predetermined. Prior to the 20th Century there was no mechanism available for this to

---

* This means that when you call a politician an empty-headed idiot, you're at least half right.

happen, but afterward a crack appeared in the cosmic egg that revealed the possibility that our transcendent or spiritual minds could control our material brains.

There was once a preacher who put this in a religious context in one of his sermons. He was well known to his congregation as a very spiritual man. So when he got up before his congregation and said in a clear voice, "I don't have a soul!", they were stunned. But then he continued and said, "I have a body. I *am* a soul."

Well, if we are eternal souls with minds that are a part of that transcendent state, does that mean that at least one of our current religions is correct? Unfortunately, science is an equal-opportunity spoil sport. A great many of the claims expressed in the Bible can't be supported given what science has revealed to us, including the great flood, the age of the world, the nature of the universe, the primacy of Adam and Eve, and the position of Earth as the center of the universe, just to mention a few.

As for the nature of Jesus of Nazareth, there are statements made in the New Testament that strongly imply that he was just a fallible human being. For example, Jesus proclaims in Mark, Matthew, and Luke that some of those listening to him will not die before the Kingdom of God arrives with power—in other words, they will witness the end of the world. That didn't happen, inspiring one theologian to remark that Christianity has based itself on that most tawdry of religious figures, an unprophetic prophet!

However, while I feel that such statements in the Bible and many more prove that Jesus was not God Incarnate, I do feel that he had an experience in the desert that fundamentally changed him. Apparently it gave him a profound insight into the human condition and an unprecedented ability to heal the most serious of illnesses. We can speculate that perhaps he had a Near Death Experience (NDE) like the ones mentioned in Moody's book. *In other words, he could have contacted the transcendent or divine nature that is present in all of us.*

But whatever the cause, it apparently happened to a human being, not to the creator of the universe masquerading as a human. If that's the case, it could happen to us if we knew how to initiate the same experience.

Here we have a problem. In order to proceed along this line of thought, we must enter the world of parapsychology, a subject which raises the hackles of many in the scientific community. Why should they take seriously a subject like Extra-Sensory Perception or ESP when it has had so much fraud, self-deception, and silliness attached to it? However, skeptics might be wise to seriously reconsider some programs that have recently demonstrated the viability of ESP, especially in the area known as Remote Viewing. One is a CIA program that has recently been declassified that listed some successes in "seeing" clandestine sites in Libya that were confirmed by reconnaissance. Another is the commercial program I mentioned in the Preface called the Silva Method that actually trains ordinary people to see and describe the illnesses of people who live miles away. In addition, another commercial program derived from the CIA program trains people to describe scenes other people are seeing while driving around the city. If people can be taught to develop their ESP, perhaps they can duplicate the experience that Jesus apparently had that changed him so profoundly.

A French Jesuit priest, Teilhard de Chardin, devoted his book, *The Phenomenon of Man*, to the theme that Jesus represented the ultimate goal of mankind. His thesis is that humanity's spiritual nature can't be considered an anomaly unrelated to the rest of the material world and that we evolve spiritually as well as materially. It is a *within-ness* that is endemic in all of nature and is evolving in its own right to produce a new being—one that is epitomized in Jesus of Nazareth. Since Teilhard as a Jesuit considered Jesus to be God Incarnate, he portrayed him as the *Omega*, the final step in the evolution of the universe planned by God from the very beginning. But if Jesus is not God, then he becomes not the final, but the next step, the *Beta*, in the evolution of our species. That would make Jesus's unvarying reference to himself as the Son of Man prophetic, indeed.

In this age of rapidly changing technology, it behooves us to attempt to achieve *Beta* ourselves before we wipe out humanity in some cataclysmic action of stupidity. While I don't agree with Teilhard that this spiritual progression is inevitable on Earth, I do think that the universe is vast and complex enough and is so designed that it is inevitable somewhere at some time. However, while the universe's immensity may assure success, it is also large enough to accommodate failure. We can't rely on the supposed automatic success of our spiritual evolution, or for that matter on some sort of divine intervention from God, to save us from ourselves.

It's up to us to make sure that that failure is not our real *Omega*. The god-like spirituality that was so evident in Jesus that his followers were inspired to turn him into God, Himself, must become manifest in all of us. As Jesus is quoted in the Gospel of Thomas found in Egypt at Nag Hammadi in 1945:

> Whoever drinks from my mouth will become as I am, and
> I will become that person, and the mysteries will be
> revealed to him.

Let's hope that this promise of a spiritual evolution for all mankind can be realized before we initiate our own catastrophic Armageddon. The chapters that follow expand on this theme and point to a possible direction that mankind could take to avoid this catastrophic failure.

****

Chapter 1 is devoted to science because it was science which seemed to prove that natural forces determined all future events. But in the past century science itself has cast doubts on the universality of determinism at the smallest levels in the physical world. Suddenly the most powerful tool we have to analyze the real nature of the universe has seemingly reversed itself and shown that the supposedly obvious deterministic nature of the world around us may be based on probabilities rather than certainties. And with a universe that started with a Big Bang the validity of a creation event has attained new credibility.

The philosophies of the 17th and 18th Centuries by the so-called Modern Philosophers have been overshadowed by the stunning success of the new scientific method. But with the recent development of Schrödinger's quantum mechanics and the evidence of the creation of the universe 13.7 billion years ago, their interesting speculations on the nature of reality take on new validity. For this reason Chapter 2 is devoted to the concepts of those philosophers who seemed to have been surprisingly prescient about the possible transcendent nature of reality.

Chapter 3 considers how the version of the physical world proposed by our current religions, primarily the Judeo/Christian religions, compare with the discoveries of science. Unfortunately the conflict between science and religion is profound and can't be ignored when considering its effect on the concept of original sin. And of course if that idea must be rejected, then it behooves us to find out the true nature of Jesus.

Chapter 4 examines what scholars think they know about the historical Jesus from examining both the canonical Gospels and the more recently discovered Gospel of Thomas. There is of course a great deal of disagreement among them, but the persuasive ideas of Albert Schweitzer that Jesus sought his own death in order to bring in the Kingdom of God are compelling. That makes Jesus a fallible human being, albeit a truly exceptional one. Without being forced to carry the mantle of God Almighty on his shoulders, Jesus's remarkable transformation in the desert following his baptism by John holds the promise of a spiritual transformation for all of us..

Chapter 5 examines Teilhard de Chardin's thesis about this transformation in detail. It parallels the discussion presented in the previous chapters in remarkable detail although from a completely different perspective. As a paleontologist Teilhard approaches the possibility of the transcendence of mankind from the point of view of an evolutionist, albeit an unconventional one. We have done so from the assumption that the dichotomy between mind and brain derives from an acceptance of our free will. But to determine what Jesus's transformation was and how it was achieved, we have to examine phenomena outside the purview of science.

Chapter 6 might be for many the most problematical of all—namely, the possible acceptance of extra-sensory perception. Since science has put to rest many of the fears generated by the Medieval concepts of ghosties and goblins and things that go bump in the night, it has also made many cast an incredulous eye to any claims of extra-sensory or miraculous events. The truth is that science does not handle anecdotal accounts very well. The stories some told in the 18th Century and before of stones falling out of the sky are typical. These tales were mocked with disdainful disbelief by the scientists of the time. Now of course meteorite falls are not only acknowledge but are considered an essential part of the creation of planets, themselves. Unfortunately when it comes to ESP, there are no metaphorical rocks that can fall on the head of a skeptic to prove their validity.

Obviously we can't blindly accept all the ridiculous off-the-wall claims of the naively credulous, but we should examine with an open mind the more serious attempts which have led to provable results. The recent disclosures of the CIA's remote viewing successes during the Cold War and the results of commercial courses to develop ESP in average people have given the effect validity. Combine this with the accounts of thousands of people who have had a near-death experience, and we might have an insight into what really happened to Jesus when he meditated in the desert.

Chapter 7 is a summing up. Why are we here? What's the purpose of our existence on Earth if we're not here because some logic-impaired super being wants to play eeney-meeney-miney-mo—"I'll reward you if you guess right, and I'll condemn you if you guess wrong?" It makes a lot more sense to assume we are in this Mixmaster called the material world in order to develop into something more than what we are. And if that's the case, then there's no reason to suppose that this is the only time we'll be here. The Hindus and Buddhists came to the same conclusion a long time ago, and as far as I'm concerned, they got that part of it right.

This 7th chapter will propose that maybe nature is designed to encourage us to move in the right direction to achieve our ultimate destiny. For millennia the proposition that there is purpose in the world has strongly appealed to both laymen and philosophers. Perhaps in this 21st Century we will actually be able to prove that this is so, not in the way that the fundamentalists and biblical literalists would like us to believe, but by understanding reality as revealed by the discoveries of science—*including Darwinian evolution*—and by understanding and developing our own transcendent natures.

If Jesus was actually resurrected from near death in the desert after he was baptized by John, his transforming experience might well be shared not only by those who have had an NDE but also by those who discover how to exploit the crack in the cosmic egg to contact their inherent transcendent nature. In other words, we are claiming that Jesus could never have achieved his stunning transformation in the desert unless it was an inherent possibility for all of humanity.

Acknowledgements

It would be impossible to acknowledge all those who have influenced my thoughts on the subjects in this book, but some who have made direct contributions in encouragement and suggestions stand out. Not the least of these, of course, is my wife of 57 years, Dottie, who has suffered through my innumerable career changes without seriously contemplating divorce, murder, or suicide. In fact, she has shown a remarkable amount of support at times when I'm sure most women would have thrown their arms up in despair, especially during the many months it took me to write this book.

My daughter, Sandy, should receive special mention for showing great courage in taking on the task of critiquing her Dad's entire book from the point of view of an interested layperson. She did not hesitate to tell me when I assumed greater knowledge of technical matters on the part of my readers than I had a right to expect, or when my attempts at humor and wit were less than successful. All authors should be so lucky to have such a fearless and competent critic to keep them on the straight and narrow.

On the technical side, there was of course Dr. Max Garbuny at Westinghouse Research Labs who inspired in me a great respect for physical research; Seth McCormick, my friend and mentor of many years who sharpened my technical writing skills; Meredith Deming and her writing-class students who provided great encouragement and suggestions for this book; and Professor Scott Brophy at Hobart College who introduced me to the Modern Philosophers of the 17th and 18th Centuries. Finally, there's my dear friend and supporter, Ann Stephenson Moe, choir director and organist at Church of the Redeemer in Sarasota, FL, who not only introduced me to some of the greatest choral music ever written, but patiently endured many of my lunch-hour pontifications about the latest chapters of this book. All of these people deserve more credit for the good aspects of this work than I can say And of course the parts that leave a great deal to be desired are mine and mine alone.

I hope you enjoy reading this as much as I did writing it and that it sheds perhaps a new light on this strange existence of ours.

Chapter 1
Science and Free Will

Determinism seems to require a lot of "double think" (defined in George Orwell's book, *1984*, as holding two mutually exclusive ideas in the mind at the same time). If every physical action is determined by natural law, then we're not in control of what we think and do. However, all the determinists that I've ever met have continued to act as if they had all the free will in the world. Double think. And of course they indulge in double think because if they were true determinists, life would become too boring and meaningless to continue. One might as well end the whole charade. But wouldn't that imply that we had free will, or was *that* decision predetermined by prior events? You can see why it's much easier for determinists to double think and say the hell with it.

The real question is, why are determinists so persistent in their belief in spite of these difficulties with it? One reason, of course, would be that the determinist didn't want to be held responsible for his or her actions. A kinder and more philosophical reason is that the incredible success of the scientific method in predicting the future wouldn't be possible if there was no predictability in natural forces. Since those forces have proven to be predictable, why wouldn't that also apply to human behavior?

Up until the 20th Century there seemed to be no reason not to believe that everything we did was determined by natural forces. But in the first few decades of the last century, science went through a revolution comparable to the Copernican of the 16th Century. It not only changed our concept of reality but it also indicated there might be a solution to the apparent dichotomy between free will and determinism.

Science and Determinism

The concept of science has been with us ever since the Greeks laid the philosophical and mathematical foundations for it more than 2400 years ago. However, until the 16th and 17th Centuries the Ptolemaic/Aristotelian model of the universe had reigned supreme for centuries and seemed to be the most obvious. It claimed that the sun, moon, stars, and planets circled the earth in concentric spheres, a situation which appeared to be confirmed simply by looking up at the sky. Unfortunately, it did not lend itself to a simple explanation for the paths of the planets, which seemed to reverse direction for short periods of time. Numerous complicated schemes were proposed to solve the problem, but none were convincing until Copernicus came up with his heliocentric model of the universe. When Francis Bacon articulated the inductive method for scientific investigations in 1620, and Galileo published his works on motion, science became what it is today.

In 1533 Nicolas Copernicus's great revolutionary work, *De Revolutionibus*,[1] was published which claimed that the earth revolved on its axis once a day and that it traveled around the sun once every year. Galileo

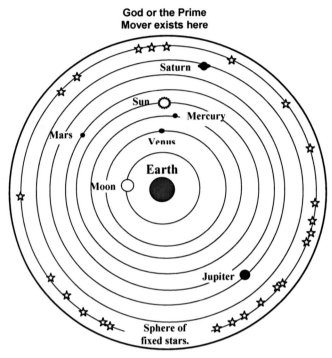

God or the Prime Mover exists here

Aristotelian/Ptolemaic
Universe

put the icing on the cake when he trained a telescope on the heavens and discovered that the moon was not a perfect sphere but had craters on it, that the planet Jupiter had moons that traveled around it, and that Venus had phases like the moon which meant that it periodically passed in back of the sun, not always in front of it like the diagram above indicates.[2] Earth, therefore, must revolve around the sun like Venus, proving that Copernicus was right. However, where Copernicus was discrete in not flaunting his concept at the Church, Galileo showed a remarkable lack of tact and implied in his *Dialogue Concerning The Two Greatest World Systems*, published in Florence in 1632, that anyone that still held to the Aristotelian concept was an idiot. Unfortunately, Pope Urban VIII was one of the idiots.

---

[1] Whose full title was *De revolutionibus orbium coelestium*, "On the revolutions of the heavenly spheres."

[2] The ancients could have come to the same conclusion without the telescope if they had noted that Venus and the Sun are *never* on opposite sides of the Earth. That's why it got its identification as the Evening and Morning star.

On Urban's command, the Roman Catholic Church, which had already burned Giordano Bruno at the stake in 1600 for challenging the official church doctrine on the structure of the universe, arrested Galileo in 1633, brought him before the dreaded Inquisition, and forced him to recant his statement that the earth revolved around the sun. It's not surprising that the Church Fathers did that, because while their actions were reprehensible, the Copernican cosmology sounded the death knell for the Church's infallibility. Once you take away Earth's central position in the universe, Biblical scripture is no longer sacrosanct, and the cosmology that put humanity at the center of the universe no longer makes any sense. Earth is now no more important than any of the other planets.

But the Church's actions were doomed to be ineffectual because the scientific technique did not depend on the claims of any individual but on the evidence. Anyone could duplicate Galileo's observations by obtaining a telescope of their own and taking a look for themselves. Some who were alive when Galileo was forced to recant lived to see Newton publish his gravitational theory and the laws of motion in 1687. Science had demonstrated its supremacy with a vengeance and an unprecedented speed. No Church could ever again hope to stop its progress.

The publication of Newton's laws changed our society in a way that is difficult for us to appreciate over 300 years later. This event wasn't just a technical triumph for science, but a profound shift in the way that even the average man or woman in the street looked at reality. Up until that time, it was thought that the motion of the heavenly objects were controlled by gods or spirits, or that the bodies, themselves, "yearned" or "desired" to follow the paths they took. It wasn't until Newton proved that gravity not only caused his mythical apple to fall on his head but also determined the motion of the heavenly bodies that people realized that natural laws, not capricious gods, controlled the universe. By simply using Newton's three laws combined with the new calculus that he invented, one could predict the precise paths of any body on Earth or in the heavens. The space program would have been impossible without Newton's laws.

It shouldn't be surprising that determinism became the reigning theory among scientists from this time up through the 19th Century. To them, nothing was accidental. If you had instruments that were accurate enough, you could determine the motion and position of every material body in the universe, even the atoms. Scientists were saying, in effect, that there was no such thing as free will.

But when we entered the 20th century, all bets were off.

Even in the 19th century there were nagging problems with the Newtonian state of things. All the planets revolve around the sun in elliptical orbits. As we said, Newton's laws faithfully predicted the paths and periodicity of all the planets—except when they came under extreme conditions. The laws couldn't predict accurately the rate of precession of Mercury, the planet closest to the Sun's huge gravitational attraction.

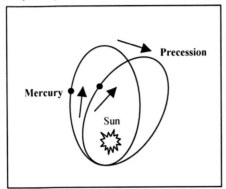

The orbit of any planet very slowly *precesses* around the sun, as shown here. The rate of precession is predicted by Newton's equations for all the planets, but is slightly off for Mercury, the planet closest to the sun.

As shown in the figure, the elliptical orbit of Mercury turns around the Sun as do the orbits of all the planets in what is called a *precession*. However, when Mercury's rate of precession was found to be slightly off; it implied that Newton's laws were not complete.

There were also problems with the way light traveled from one place to another. James Clerk Maxwell showed in the famous *Maxwell Equations* that moving magnets and electric currents generated fields which created each other. These fields also do not travel instantly from one place to another as Newton supposed, but move at a definite velocity. And since a moving magnetic field can create an electric current that in turn creates a magnetic field, an undulating wave can be created with each effect alternately creating the other. To his surprise, he determined that the speed of the wave was identical to the speed of light, indicating that light itself was an electro-magnetic phenomenon. But if light was an electro-magnetic wave, what was the medium that was waving?

The prevailing theory was that an invisible *aether* (or *ether*) provided the medium by which light traveled through space just like sound waves travel through the air. But as the planet Earth moved through the aether, the speed of light should vary depending on the direction you measure it on the moving earth. If you measured it while shining light in the direction the earth was traveling relative to the aether, it should take more time for the beam to go from one place to the next, like a boat going upstream, than if you measured at right angles to the direction of motion. Unfortunately, a brilliant experiment by Michelson and Morley proved conclusively that the speed of light remained constant, no matter in what direction the earth was moving relative to the supposed aether. When the Michelson-Morley experiment implied that there was no aether, scientists looked for some way out of this dilemma.

Hendrik Lorentz (1853-1928) and George Fitzgerald (1851-1901) independently proposed a mathematical solution in 1892 that could account for the null result of the Michelson-Morley experiment while retaining the existence of the aether. Lorentz created some equations based on a suggestion made by Fitzgerald that showed that if matter contracted by just the right amount when moving through the aether, it would be impossible to detect a variation in the speed of light and consequently the presence of the aether. However, this *Lorentz contraction* was an *ad hoc* solution created by manipulating some mathematical equations—they were not derived from a known physical effect of the aether. In addition, if such a contraction was caused by the aether, the latter had to be resistant enough to make matter contract when moving through it, but so non-resistant at the same time that no appreciable drag could be detected when it did. The stars and planets moved through space as if there was nothing resisting their movements, as if they moved through a vacuum. The aether couldn't accomplish both effects simultaneously.

Einstein reversed the classical viewpoint by eliminating the aether and proposing that there was no variation in the speed of light to detect. It was simply a universal constant just as Maxwell's equations implied. By doing this he was able to show that the so-called *Lorentz contraction* is not due to an actual deformation of bodies traveling through a non-existent aether, but to a change in the way space and time are measured when you assume that the speed of light never varies. With that assumption Einstein *derived* the Lorentz equations which were incorporated into his Special Theory of Relativity.

Einstein's equations also indicated that mass and energy are interchangeable—in the famous equation $E = mc^2$—and that space and time are inseparable. Energy then becomes the equivalent of mass and what we now call the space-time continuum extends throughout the visible universe.

The Special Theory of Relativity involved the speed of two frames of reference, called inertial frames, that were moving relative to each other at a constant velocity close to the speed of light. When Einstein considered frames of reference that were accelerating, he created a theory of gravitation, now called the General Theory of Relativity, which predicted among other things that light would bend when it passed by a massive body like the sun because the sun would distort the space-time continuum around it. When astronomers aimed their telescopes at the sun during a total eclipse and measured the position of stars whose light passed very close to the sun's edge, they proved that the light did bend due to the sun's distortion of space, thus supporting Einstein's theory of the space-time continuum.

Now it might seem that the problems of the precession of the elliptical orbit of Mercury and the absence of the aether didn't have very much to do with the supposed deterministic nature of reality, but when Einstein solved both of them with his two theories, it made those who believed in determinism a little nervous because Newton's Laws did not seem to be universal.[3]   However, most scientists felt that they would just have to consider these relativity matters when they predicted the exact future of all events in the universe. Determinism wasn't dead, it was just harder to calculate!

But the weird had entered the nice, neat, Newtonian universe. Consider for example Special Relativity's primary assumption that the speed of light is constant throughout the universe, no matter how rapidly or slowly the source moves in relation to the measuring instrument. That's a concept that Newtonian physicists would (and did) find hard to swallow. If

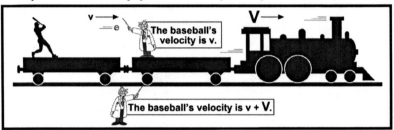

someone, Sam, on a train moving at a velocity V measures the velocity of a baseball hit in the same direction to be v, another observer, Harry, standing along side of the tracks would measure the velocity of the baseball as the velocity Sam measured plus the velocity of the train, or v + V. Everything makes sense and all's right with the Newtonian universe.

Yet Einstein was saying that if Sam was sending a beam of light in the direction the train was traveling, both Sam and Harry would measure its velocity as c. Harry might be expected to measure the speed of light to be $V + c$, but even if the train were traveling close to the speed of light, he would still measure it to be c instead of c + c or 2c. Nothing makes sense and all is *not* right with the Newtonian universe.

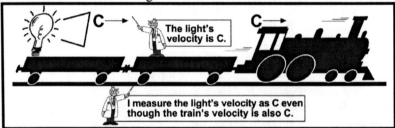

The consequences of this are very strange, indeed. In order to explain this in a logical manner, and all scientists insist that logic must

---

[3]   A headline in *The Times* of London on November 8, 1919, proclaimed, "The Revolution in Science—Einstein Versus Newton." Actually Einstein's Special Theory equations do not conflict with Newton's but are simply a more complete version of Newton's Laws, because when you deal with speeds much slower than the speed of light, the Einstein equations reduce to Newton's. However, the tenor of the headline reflects the real concern that scientists must have felt at the time.

prevail, one has to assume that the clocks used by Sam and Harry to measure the speed of the beam of light are not running at the same rate.[4] Sam will say that Harry's clock was running too fast, while Harry would say that Sam's clock was too slow. Suddenly, time itself was no longer universal for everyone, as the Newtonians always assumed, but relative.

For example, consider the twin paradox: Suppose our friend Sam has decided to go on a spaceship that can attain a speed close to the speed of light to a star system called 55-Cancri that is 41 light years away and seems to have three large planets similar to our Jupiter, Saturn, and Neptune. Sam's identical twin brother, George, is less adventuresome and stays on Earth. When Sam returns home, Sam will find that George is either dead or about 80 years older than he is. The reason for this is that Sam's time has slowed down as he traveled close to the speed of light in comparison to George's time.

It may seem that there should be no difference between the times of the two since George would be moving away from Sam at the same speed that Sam would be moving away from George. The difference lies in the fact that energy has been applied to Sam's spaceship to *accelerate* it to near light speed. That acceleration slows down Sam's time compared to George's time because no energy has been applied to George's "spaceship," Earth.

For the length of time that Sam would be traveling at this speed, Sam would be getting older at a much slower rate than George. When Sam decelerated at his destination, his time would return to the same rate as George's while he messed around at the star system. Once he accelerated again to come home to Earth, his time would again slow down to practically nothing until he landed and matched Earth's time-rate once more.[5]

The success of these concepts was getting more and more troublesome for classical Newtonian physicists and their belief in determinism. If Newton's Laws are not applicable in these extreme cases, that implies that the concept of determinism may also be on slippery ground. Unfortunately, for both classical physics and determinism the worst was yet to come.

One of the problems that plagued the classical world of physics was the behavior of the atom. Atoms were assumed to be little hunks of matter that combined with other hunks of matter to form molecules which

---

[4] One of the phenomena which proved this was true involved gamma ray bombardment of the Earth's upper atmosphere. Gamma rays, the most powerful radiation striking Earth, produce particles called muons in the atmosphere which have a very short lifetime, much too short to last until they hit the ground. The fact that we can detect them at ground level proves that their extreme velocity has slowed their "clocks" enough so that they can exist until they reach the earth.

[5] As far as we know, this is the only way that anyone can time travel, and it can only be done in one direction; namely, to the future. And since we've seen no visitors from the future, the chances that we will ever be able to travel into the past are slim.

made up the structure of the universe. In fact, based on the work done in the 1890's by Cavendish scientist J. J. Thompson, the popular image of the atom at that time was of a pseudo-solid permeable mass with electrons dotted within it, somewhat like the raisins in a British raisin pudding. Even though the negative electrons would repel each other, the "pudding" part of the atom was assumed to be positive to hold the whole thing together and result in an electrically neutral atom.

Raisin-pudding atom with negative electrons scattered in the positive "pudding."

But then a student of Thompson's, Ernest Rutherford, conducted an experiment in 1911 that literally changed the course of science. Rutherford, a New Zealander who had traveled to Cambridge to join Thompson at the Cavendish, had made some significant discoveries about radioactive substances. He discovered that at least two types of emissions come from radioactive materials: alpha rays and beta rays. Alpha particles are identical to the positive helium nuclei, consisting of two protons and two neutrons, and can be used to bombard a target to determine if any positive subatomic particle in the target can deflect it. With the British raisin pudding concept of the atom, he and his assistants expected that a thin gold foil would allow most of the particles to pass straight through while deflecting a few slightly off course. To their astonishment, about one particle in 8,000 *was deflected 45 degrees or more, some coming directly back to the source*! Rutherford said, "It was almost as incredible as if you fired a 15-inch Naval shell at a piece of tissue paper, and the shell came right back and hit you." Raisin pudding, indeed!

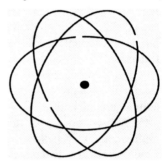

Orbiting-electron atom with almost all the mass in the positive core. An electron is 1/5000 the mass of the nuclear core.

Eventually Rutherford proved that in order for these events to occur, almost all of the mass and all of the positive energy must be concentrated in a central nucleus about 10,000 times smaller in diameter than that of the entire atom. In order to balance the positive charge and produce a neutral atom, an electrical charge must be orbiting the nucleus at the circumference of the space that comprised the atom. In other words, matter is almost all empty space[6] with the fields of energy repelling other atoms from entering, thereby creating the illusion of solidity. The once solid Newtonian universe was beginning to look very ephemeral, indeed.

This planetary model of the atom had already been proposed in 1904 by Hantaro Nagaoka, a Japanese physicist, but rejected because according to classical physics, electrons orbiting in the electrical field of the nucleus would radiate their energy and fall almost immediately into the central nucleus, making it impossible for any material in the universe to exist. But the results of Rutherford could not be denied and the world of physics was in turmoil until in 1913 Danish physicist, Neils Bohr, proposed only remaining logical consistency with the facts; namely, that classical physics was wrong and that for some reason negative electrons rotating about a positive core did *not* radiate energy. In fact, he suggested that they emitted or absorbed energy only when they *jumped* from one "permitted" orbit to another, which explained some other facts which had been puzzling classical physicists for some time.

It was a tenet of classical physics that all radiation was continuous, progressing smoothly from one frequency to the next. However, this did not jibe with some experiments in heat and light which were extremely puzzling. For instance, when the light emitted by a burning material was passed through a spectrometer or prism,[7] it was not continuous but displayed discrete dark absorption bands or lines at unique frequencies for each substance. In fact, by determining the spectrum of each of the elements, one could determine the composition of any radiating substance, like the sun or any other star, by identifying the frequency of each of the bands in its spectrum.

Bohr's orbit-hopping electrons seemed to explain these discrete bands nicely. Each time an electron absorbs an energy quantum of a specific frequency, it will create a dark absorption line by jumping to a higher energy level. And when it drops from one energy level to a lower one, it emits an energy "quantum" of the same frequency creating a bright line. When elements have a number of electrons in a number of different orbits (i.e., at different energy levels), they will produce different spectrum lines that identify the element and precisely define the energy of each orbiting electron.

---

[6] As we pointed out in the Introduction, if the nucleus were the size of a golf ball and placed in the center of a football stadium, the electrons would be less than the size of a gnat, circling it at the perimeter of the stadium.

[7] As any high-school science enthusiast can tell you, a prism will break up a beam of white light into a rainbow of colors. Spectrometers incorporate a prism and a microscope so that operators can examine the rainbow, or spectrum, in detail. When they do so, they will detect lines or bands at different points along the spectrum representing different light frequencies, from the highest frequencies in blue to the lowest in red.

This model of the atom worked well for hydrogen and singly ionized helium but not for atoms containing more than one electron. In 1926 Edwin Schrödinger developed a *new quantum mechanics* based on the principle proposed by Louis de Broglie that matter and energy were *wave-particles*—i.e., both waves and particles at the same time—and on the Heisenberg *uncertainty principle*. Schrödinger's new quantum mechanics was highly successful in describing not only the properties of the hydrogen atom, but also of more complicated systems—atoms, molecules, and metals. Indeed, if it weren't for quantum mechanics, there would be no laser beams, integrated circuits, computer chips, superconducting materials, and a host of other modern developments.

The Heisenberg uncertainty principle states that it is impossible to determine the momentum and position of a subatomic particle at the same time. If you know the position of a subatomic particle accurately, then you would have no knowledge of its subsequent momentum (calculated by multiplying its mass and velocity). If the exact position and momentum of particles cannot be known simultaneously, no one can predict the effect of a given cause in the subatomic world. In the 20th century, therefore, physics moved from a world of precision and predictability to one of chance and probability for subatomic particles.

The idea proposed by de Broglie that a particle was both a wave and a particle at the same time was the result of experiments which showed energy waves behaving like particles and particles behaving like waves. The most spectacular of these was a modification of an experiment that seemed to prove that light was definitely wavelike.

Called Young's experiment, it consisted of sending light from a single light source through two adjacent narrow slits to a wall or target (see below). If one of the slits was covered, a simple ordinary light pattern resulted with the brightest part in the center, gradually falling off on two sides. When both slits were opened, a light pattern of alternating light and

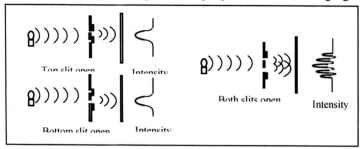

Young's experiment showed that light must be wavelike because only waves could interfere to produce light and dark bands with 2 open slits.

dark lines formed where the light waves emerging from the slits alternately enhanced and canceled each other out. This could only be explained if light was wavelike in nature, with the wave from one slit interacting with the wave from the other. When the crest of one wave coincided with the crest of the other, a bright line would result. But when the trough of one wave coincided with the crest of the other, they would cancel each other out causing a dark line to appear. Therefore the wave theory was the prevailing one for light until the 20th century.

However, Einstein and Bohm proved that light could also be described as particles or "photons" of energy, $h\nu$, where h was a very small quantity called Plank's Constant, and ν was the light's frequency. [8] But how could this be reconciled with Young's experiment which proved that light was wavelike in character? In an attempt to find out what was going on, it was decided to conduct a split screen experiment with individual photons. But when experimenters diminished the light intensity drastically so that only one photon of light at a time passed through one slit or the other in a seemingly random pattern, the same alternating light and dark pattern emerged over a period of time, as if the light particles "knew" where they were supposed to go to create an interference wave pattern, as shown below, that could only be understood if the single photon passed through both slits at the same time or somehow realized that there were two slits instead of one.

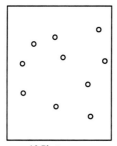

10 Photons

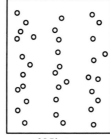

35 Photons

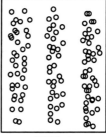

120 Photons

This didn't make any sense at all. How could the individual photons "know" that there was another slit "over there" that would cause it to impinge on only certain "permitted" areas of the target screen? There were presumably no waves accompanying the photons which could cross each other and add or subtract their amplitudes to form the bands of light.

This experiment established the particle-wave nature of matter along with some diffraction experiments with electrons and opened the door to the Copenhagen Interpretation and the demise of predetermination at the subatomic level.

But does that also leave the door open for free will?

---

[8] In fact, Einstein received the Nobel prize in physics because of this discovery, not for his Theory of Relativity.

The Copenhagen Interpretation

The Copenhagen Interpretation is a fanciful name for a decision made by two of our previously mentioned physicists, Neils Bohr and Werner Heisenberg, while in Copenhagen in 1927. There could be no doubt that there had to be some sort of explanation about the dual nature of these microscopic particles. How can it be possible to have something that is both a particle and a wave at the same time? Particles bounce off one another while a couple of waves can pass through each other, cancel each other out, or add their amplitudes.

The purpose of the Copenhagen Interpretation was the resolution of these seemingly contradictory states. In essence Bohr and Heisenberg maintained that the particle and wave nature of matter were "complimentary" with one another, and only one or the other would manifest itself when the experimenter chose which to observe in an experiment! In other words, a particle was both a particle and a wave until one or the other attribute was used in an experiment.

A contemporary physicist, Michio Kaku, put it in religious terms like this: "According to traditional Judaic-Christian thought, we have something called determinism...God is omniscient. The quantum principle upsets the entire apple cart. If God cannot know where the electron is, he cannot know what a human being will do or feel in the future. Free will is reintroduced into our world." So it isn't just the traditional scientists whose favored preconceptions are being challenged, but the conventional Judaic-Christian theologian's as well.

Kaku has pointed out something that I once heard a priest proclaim in a sermon. He said that if we say that we have the free will to either save ourselves by following the teachings of Jesus or condemn ourselves to a godless life by refusing to do so, *then we can't claim that God is omnipotent*! His argument didn't rely on the quantum principle as Kaku's did, but on the simple logic that our freedom of choice implies that God is leaving it up to us to make a decision. If we had the free will to make our own decisions, then God doesn't choose to exercise the power to force us to make them the way He wants us to. Why? Obviously, because the outcome He desires requires us to make up our own minds. According to the stories in the Bible and the traditional approach that all religions have taken to the problem, not just the Christian churches, we must decide for ourselves which path to follow. But that means that He can't do it for us. Thus God is not omnipotent, because even if you say He chooses not to use His power, that power apparently isn't omnipotent since He can't force the outcome to come out the way He wants it to without our help! Needless to say this did not sit well with many in the congregation nor with any of the resident priests.

The far reaching result of the Copenhagen concept is that events depend on the presence and observation of an observer. While it was hotly debated between Bohr and Albert Einstein, inspiring the latter to make his famous statement that "God does not play dice with the universe," the viability of quantum mechanics is unquestioned by all scientists, and the Copenhagen Interpretation has become accepted by a significant number. While Werner Heisenberg and Neils Bohr originally viewed their interpretation as a limitation on experimental techniques when X-ray detection disturbed the velocity and position of subatomic particles, they quickly came to believe it described an indeterminacy in the very nature of the microcosmic world.[9] However, this suggests that if the nature of events in the subatomic world depends on the fact that someone sees them happen, why wouldn't that fact also apply at the macrocosmic level? Why didn't the existence of all that we see in the material world depend on our observing it?

One of those who wanted to show that this concept was ridiculous was the author of quantum mechanics, himself—Erwin Schrödinger.

Enter Schrödinger's Cat

Perhaps the best way to explain the paradox of Schrödinger's cat is to let the author of the paradox tell you in his own words. The following is an excerpt from the paper given by Schrödinger in 1935:

> One can even set up quite ridiculous cases. A cat is penned up in a steel chamber, along with the following diabolical device (which must be secured against direct interference by the cat): in a Geiger counter there is a tiny bit of radioactive substance, so small that perhaps in the course of one hour one of the atoms decays, but also, with equal probability, perhaps none; if it happens, the counter tube discharges and through a relay releases a hammer which shatters a small flask of hydro-cyanic acid. If one has left this entire system to itself for an hour, one would say that the cat still lives if meanwhile no atom has decayed. The first atomic decay would have poisoned it. The Psi function for the entire system would express this by having in it the living and the deadcat (pardon the expression) mixed or smeared out in equal parts.[10]

---

[9] That's because it is just as impossible to predict when a radioactive material will emit a particle as it is to actively determine the particle's position and momentum at the same time. The event is detected by a passive detector and not disturbed by the experimenter's examination.

[10] That is, the cat would be both living and dead at the same time until someone opened the box and looked at it, at which point the cat would revert to one state or the other!

It is typical of these cases that an indeterminacy originally restricted to the atomic domain becomes transformed into macroscopic indeterminacy, which can then be resolved by direct observation. That prevents us from so naively accepting as valid a "blurred model" for representing reality. In itself it would not embody anything unclear or contradictory.[11]

Although Schrödinger's thought experiment was his attempt to point out that we can't assume that microscopic indeterminacy implies a "blurring" of reality because it would lead to ridiculous conclusions, it has actually been used to support the idea that our material world is indeterminate until it is observed by humans, a concept remarkably similar to a philosophy put forward by an 18th century cleric, Bishop Berkeley, as we will see in the next chapter.

What does this mean as far as determinism and free will are concerned? While it is true that the thought processes of living beings occurs in neurons and synapses that are many orders of magnitude greater than subatomic particles, does this mean that thought itself is unaffected by the uncertainty principle? And although some scientists vigorously deny that the uncertainty principle proves that free will is possible, it's hard to overlook the implications that thought could be directed by some sort of "willing" mechanism in our center of consciousness.

If Free Will is Real, Where is it Coming From?

If you believe as the materialists do that there is nothing other than the physical, material universe, then you would have to come to the conclusion that if uncertainty were present in our thought patterns, it's hard to imagine that thought itself would not be random. Since thought is obviously not random and since materialists can't admit that there might be something other than the material world, the only conclusion that they can draw is that even though the uncertainty principle might apply to the subatomic particles in the neurons and synapses of the brain, somehow when the trillions of subatomic particles get together, certainty reemerges in the brain and free will disappears.

For the rest of us, Occam's Razor may offer a more satisfying conclusion. William of Occam, a 14th century logician and Franciscan friar, stated the principle that "Entities should not be multiplied unnecessarily."[12] This became known as Occam's Razor which "cut away" elaborate and complex solutions in preference for the simplest. Now the determinists might think it is much simpler to wave their hands and say that something

---

[11] Schrödinger, Erwin, Translator: John D. Trimmer, "The Present Situation in Quantum Mechanics," *Proceedings of the American Philosophical Society*, 1935, 124, 323-28.

[12] Or in the words of the modern acronym, KISS: "Keep it simple, stupid."

"natural" is going on that we can't identify as the seat of consciousness, but I doubt that Occam had ignorance of a cause as an example of a simpler solution. How about this instead: If nothing in the physical world can precisely determine the actions of subatomic particles, and since thought is most likely a subatomic phenomenon and can obviously be directed logically by sentient human beings, then there's probably something non-physical directing thought. We're back to Sherlock's dictum: "...when you have eliminated the impossible, whatever remains, *however improbable, must be the truth.*"

It will take many years before we will know if this assumption is really correct. One possible way we can prove that the theory is *incorrect* would be to create consciousness in our closest replica of a human brain—the computer. That is, we will know whether or not a physical model combined with the proper sophisticated software can bring matter to intelligent, sentient life. If we can, then we will have to throw free will into the trash because it will mean that in spite of the uncertainty principle all actions are determined by natural laws.

That paradox, which implies that the human species can and must conduct an experiment that will prove it can't do what it just did without being predetermined to do so, will have been proven to be correct.

I don't buy it and in a sense neither does Roger Penrose, the celebrated mathematician who shared the internationally prestigious Wolf Prize with Stephen Hawking for their work on the beginnings of the universe.

Roger Penrose and the Seat of Consciousness

Penrose has written two books that deal in great detail with the question of the nature of the seat of consciousness, *The Emperor's New Mind* and *Shadows of the Mind*. The former is a comprehensive survey of quantum mechanics, the brain, and the computational limitations of computers. The *Shadows of the Mind* is essentially an attempt to answer the objections that Penrose's peers raised against the arguments presented in the first book and calls for the creation of a "new science" to explain how a human's seat of consciousness can be the product of the physical brain. Make no mistake, Penrose is a materialist through and through, and even joins Einstein in his conviction that quantum mechanics is an incomplete theory that needs a great deal of "fixing up." However, he is at great pains to explain why he believes that it will be impossible for scientists to create a sentient computer—one that could exhibit self-awareness—as he states in the concluding chapter of *The Emperor's New Mind*:

> In this book I have presented many arguments intending to show the untenability of the viewpoint—apparently rather prevalent in current philosophizing—that our

thinking is basically the same as the action of some very complicated computer...

Some readers may...have regarded the 'strong-[Artificial-Intelligence] supporter' as perhaps largely a straw man! Is it not 'obvious' that mere computation cannot evoke pleasure or pain; that it cannot perceive poetry or the beauty of an evening sky or the magic of sounds; that it cannot hope or love or despair; that it cannot have a genuine autonomous purpose? Yet science seems to have driven us to accept that we are all merely small parts of a world governed in full detail (even if perhaps ultimately just problematically) by very precise mathematical laws...Perhaps when computations become extraordinarily complicated they can begin to take on the more poetic or subjective qualities that we associate with the term "mind." *Yet it is hard to avoid an uncomfortable feeling that there must always be something missing from such a picture.* [Emphasis mine.]

In my own arguments I have tried to support this view that there must indeed be something essential that is missing from any purely computational picture. Yet I hold also to the hope that it is through science and mathematics that some profound advances in the understanding of mind must eventually come to light...

Consciousness seems to me to be such an important phenomenon that I simply cannot believe that it is something just "accidentally" conjured up by a complicated computation...[13]

That's pretty far out for a scientist-mathematician to claim. And as I said, it appears that the scientific community brought him to task for it because he apparently felt it was necessary to defend his position in the sequel, *Shadows of the Mind.* He tries to avoid the implication that science can't reproduce consciousness by dividing its cause into four different categories:

A. All thinking is computations; in particular, feelings of conscious awareness are evoked merely by the carrying out of appropriate computations.

B. Awareness is a feature of the brain's physical action; and whereas any physical action can be simulated

---

[13] Penrose, Roger; *The Emperor's New Mind,* Oxford University Press, 1989, p. 579.. By permission of Oxford University Press

computationally, computational simulation cannot by itself evoke awareness.

C. Appropriate physical action of the brain evokes awareness, but this physical action cannot even be properly simulated computationally.

D. Awareness cannot be explained by physical, computational, or any other scientific terms. [14]

Viewpoint *A* is the one taken by the "strong-Artificial-Intelligence supporter" mentioned in the first quote, while *D* is the exact opposite, the view of the "strong-non-AI supporter." In between Penrose attempts a fine-tuning of the possible viewpoints of consciousness between these two extremes.

In my opinion viewpoint *B* is a most peculiar argument. If awareness results from a physical action and "any physical action can be simulated computationally," then it seems to be logically inconsistent for anyone to claim that "computational simulation cannot by itself evoke awareness" when it has already been claimed that awareness is a physical activity that can be simulated. On the other hand, what he's really saying here is that something "outside" physical reality is causing the brain to become self aware because computation *by itself* cannot cause it. If he accepted that position, it would imply that he believed that there is a transcendent dimension that our physical computation laws can't manipulate because by definition it can't be a part of "physical" reality.

Viewpoint *C* is a clearer statement of his dilemma. Penrose is in the same position that an intelligent 17th century theologian might have been in when he examined the Copernican/Galilean model of the universe that claimed that the Earth and the other planets revolved around the sun. The ancient cleric could put a telescope to his eye and see the moons revolving around Jupiter, and since our moon obviously revolved around us, the earth was no different from any other planet. Just as the poor theologian knew that his religion was not based on a real cosmology, so must Penrose realize that there is something which is beyond the power of his science to explain. Viewpoint *C* is his statement that although there is no way that science can explain consciousness, surely there must be a "new" science out there waiting to be discovered which will explain how consciousness can be the sole result of the brain's physical, material activity. Unfortunately, it appears that this new science must be a function of a transcendent world since by his own admission, it can't be a part of this physical world.

---

[14] Penrose, Roger; *Shadows of the Mind*, Oxford University Press, 1994, p. 12. By permission of Oxford University Press.

It was implied earlier that Roger Penrose does not hold with the classical deterministic point of view, but the truth is that he thinks there must be a different type of determinism that denies the possibility of free will. [15] For instance, as we can see here, he definitely does not want to accept his fourth viewpoint: "*D. Awareness cannot be explained by physical, computational, or any other scientific terms.*" Penrose attempts to get around this self-imposed dilemma by saying that non-computability does not mean non-determinism, a point of view he goes to great pains to try to prove throughout his book. But this is just the same as saying that there must be a new way to do science because computability uses the same tools that our current science uses. In other words, this is a faith statement because he wants to believe that such a new science is possible without any practical evidence that it is.

So it looks like we're back to Occam's Razor.

The value of both Penrose's books to this discussion is that he has presented a powerful and compelling scientific and mathematical analysis of consciousness and has come to the conclusion that there is no way that science can explain *or reproduce it*! Consciousness is something outside physical reality and is therefore not subject to the same determinability that applies to physical, macroscopic objects. And the point of entry, so to speak, of the mind into the brain is very likely at the subatomic level where determinability no longer applies and free will can reign supreme.

But if we have free will, what is its purpose? A lot depends on whether or not there is some intelligence out there that started the whole business going. Indeed, until only a half century ago, according to most scientists there was no real need to believe in an eternal God if you already had an eternal universe. No creation means no creator; no creator means no God.

Was the Universe Created?

The first cracks to appear in the idea of an eternal, infinite universe came in 1823 when Olber's Paradox was proposed: "Why is the night sky so dark?" If the stars were evenly distributed throughout space and were everywhere, the whole sky should be brilliantly bright. There shouldn't be any night at all.

There seemed to be only three ways to explain why the night was dark: (1) stars are not everywhere in the universe and our line of sight eventually runs out of stars to see, (2) the universe was very young, or (3)

---

[15] As we have seen, Penrose agrees that creating an intelligent computer with its own consciousness is currently impossible. But as far as free will is concerned, he says that "...free will...would have to be intimately tied in with some non-computable ingredient in the laws that govern the world in which we actually live." Sounds like he's agreeing with us since transcendence would certainly qualify as "some non-computable ingredient."

the universe was expanding and the light from the distant stars hadn't had enough time to reach us.

None of these solutions were very comforting to scientists who believed in an eternal, infinite universe. If the universe was infinite and uniform, stars should be everywhere. If the universe was young, that meant it was created at a finite time in the past, which was also true if the universe was expanding. This was certainly troubling to scientists, but they were convinced that the paradox wasn't troubling enough to cause them to drop the idea of an infinite, eternal universe.

However, a little over a half century ago an event occurred that provided new evidence to support the idea that the universe had a definite beginning. Edwin Hubble discovered something called the *red shift*, and the eternal universe idea was immediately put into very serious jeopardy.

The Big Bang

Hubble first discovered that the so-called *nebulae* which astronomers assumed were clouds of gas within our own Milky Way or "island universe" (galaxy) actually contained stars and were other galaxies many millions or billions of light years away from us. In addition, the light emitted by those galaxies was shifted toward the red end of the spectrum. And the farther away the galaxies the greater the shift, which implied that the galaxies were moving away from each other.

The reason for this was because of an effect which was discovered by Austrian mathematician and physicist Christian Doppler in the mid 19th century. When an ambulance goes by you, the siren's pitch changes from high to low. That's because the sound waves passing your ear are going faster (at a higher frequency) when the source is coming towards you and slower (at a lower frequency) when it's going away. The same is also true of light waves, but light has such a high frequency and velocity that we don't notice the effect until it involves the great distances and speeds of the galaxies. Then when the star is moving away, the light spectrum shifts towards the red or lower frequencies, just like the sound waves drop to a lower pitch when the ambulance has passed and is going away. Since the amount of light-shift to the red is directly proportional to the distance of the stars and galaxies from us, the further away they are, the faster they travel, which is what one would expect if the universe started with a huge explosion. Thus it has become known as the *Big Bang* theory of the origin of the universe.

The reason this causes so much consternation on the part of the scientists is that it necessarily implies that something or someone created the explosion and therefore created the universe. Many scientists abhor this idea because the one thing they don't want is a Supreme Being mucking about with their physical laws. The field of science depends totally on the repeatability of phenomena. If you have a Super Power lurking outside the universe, what's to prevent It from sticking Its finger into some physical phenomenon and making it behave differently on Tuesdays, Thursdays, and Saturdays than it does on Mondays, Wednesdays, and Fridays?

Since the evidence certainly seems to indicate otherwise, the search was on for some other explanation for the Red Shift.

Before we go any further, it might be profitable for us to examine how scientists go about the business of proving or disproving a theory. When scientists are really working at their craft and not palming off a pet theory of theirs on some gullible TV personalities, they can't just have pretty pictures created on a TV screen and talk their way out of an unpleasant objection to their theory. They've either got to show that the data which led to the theory they disliked was incorrect or corrupted in some fashion, or come up with a new theory that explains the facts in a more acceptable manner to them while still adhering to the previously verified laws of science and mathematics. And most fundamental of all, they must submit their findings to the review of their peers, who would be all too happy to point out any errors in observation or computation.

In the case of the red shift, no matter how many measurements they took, they couldn't fault Hubble, who was an extremely careful and qualified astronomer. The red shift was really there and it definitely indicated that the universe was expanding. So they had to turn to their second option and come up with a new theory that explained the facts but preserved the idea that the universe was eternal and not "created" at some specific point in time.

An Attempt to Retain the Infinite, Eternal Universe

A number of theories were put forward, but the one that seemed to have the greatest chance for success was the Steady State Theory initially proposed by Sir James Jeans around 1920 and expanded by Hermann Bondi, Thomas Gold, and Sir Fred Hoyle in 1948. Basically, the theory stated that matter was being created and destroyed everywhere so that the average cosmic density remained constant. According to the theory new matter in the form of hydrogen is being created all the time at a rate of about one hydrogen atom every 50 million years in a space about the size of a large house. Unfortunately, this rate is far too slow to be detectable by any current method.

However, this means that we should see stars and galaxies in the same mixture of ages all over the universe, an effect described as the *perfect cosmological principle*. But in fact, the further away that stellar matter is, the younger it is with no indication that old and young matter are equally mixed. In the 1960s quasars were discovered which emitted an incredible amount of light billions of light-years away from us, which means they existed billions of years in the past. Nothing in the closer, more recent universe even approximates their brilliance. So the *perfect cosmological principle* that the universe looks essentially the same from every spot in it and at every moment in time was wrong. In addition, the theory violates the conservation of matter and energy which states that no mass/energy can be created or destroyed in the universe. Still the Steady State theorists hung on hoping against hope that some new twist in the theory could account for these pesky problems.

Alas, such was not to be the case. In 1964 Princeton astrophysicist Bob Dicke realized that the Big Bang would produce microwave radio waves and the remnant of those waves should be present even now because of the intense heat of the original event. At the same time two radio astronomers at the Bell Labs thirty miles away, Robert Wilson and Arno Penzias, were working on a giant horn antenna, intended for tracking satellites. Unfortunately, it was picking up an extremely annoying background noise no matter in which direction the horn was pointing. Eliminating every possible cause, including the pigeon droppings from a couple of pigeons occupying the antenna,[16] the two scientists in desperation gave Dicke a call to see if he could help explain the reason for the phenomenon. Dicke realized instantly that he and his team had been too slow in getting their own antenna up and working and said to them, "Boys we've been scooped." Wilson and Penzias had accidentally discovered the remnants of the mighty explosion which marked the beginning of the universe. Admittedly at 3 degrees Kelvin it was only a whisper of the billions of degrees that marked the beginning temperature of the Big Bang, but it was enough because nothing in the Steady State theory could explain it. Only the intense density of the original condition of a Big Bang universe could account for the remnant energy.

Penzias and Wilson in front of their horn antenna at Bell Laboratories.

An interesting sidebar to this is that both Wilson and Penzias were Steady State enthusiasts and would have loved to see that theory vindicated as much as Bondi, Gold, and Hoyle. But in the face of the unquestionable finding of their own experiment they were forced to abandon their firmly held beliefs. Such is the way of science and the reason for its stunning success in our pursuit of knowledge. Faith and belief may motivate a scientist to devote years of intense research along a particular line of inquiry, but only hard evidence obtained on the anvil of repeatable

---

[16] In fact the pigeon trap is on display at the Smithsonian Museum.

experimentation or observation will move the scientific community to share in that faith and belief. The status of the person proposing the theory *and the attractiveness of the theory itself* counts for nothing.

Back to the Very Beginning...and End

With the Big Bang theory seeming to be the only theory that could account for all the facts, scientists turned their attention to the age of the universe and its ultimate destiny. Extrapolating backward from the current estimate of the rate of expansion of the universe, it appears that the primary explosion must have occurred about 13.7 billion years ago. The details at the very beginning of the universe will also interest us, but for the moment let's take a look at the universe's ultimate destiny.

According to Einstein's General Theory of Relativity there are three scenarios for the end of the universe, depending on the amount of mass it has. As the universe expands, the gravitational attraction of the mass within it constantly slows it down. If there is enough mass, the expansion will slowly come to a stop and then start to contract all the way down to its original point in what has been called "the big crunch." If there is too little mass, the universe will continue to expand forever until all energy in it is exhausted and there is nothing left but drifting rocks. The third possibility is that the balance between the expansive force of the original explosion and the retarding force of gravity is so balanced that it keeps slowing down forever but never completely stopping. The first is called the "closed" (spherically shaped) universe, the second is called an "open" (saddle-like shaped) universe, and the third is called a "flat " universe with a shape between the spherical and saddle.

The first and third possibilities give scientists back their eternal universe, but not very satisfactorily. The big crunch gives the best possibilities because it implies that maybe the universe has been exploding and contracting forever, sort of like a yo-yo universe. The only problem is that in 1983 and 1984 Marc Sher, Alan Guth, and Sidney Bludman demonstrated that in effect the contraction should be called "the big plop" rather than the big crunch because there wouldn't be enough energy to cause it to explode again. It would act more like a lump of clay when dropped on a hard surface—just "plop."

As for the universe that keeps slowing down but never stopping, that certainly results in an eternal universe, but what keeps everything from slowly decaying to that great equilibrium predicted by the theory of entropy? The latter says that there can only be an increase in randomness or equilibrium as time goes on, not a decrease. A lump of ice in a cup of coffee eventually melts so that the coffee attains a temperature between its original lip-scalding one and the freezing temperature of the ice cube. So too the universe will eventually cool down to the absolute zero of space.

Time will certainly continue without stopping, but who cares? Dead is dead, eternal or not.

What Happened at the Beginning?

What was the nature of the original *primordial atom* that created the universe? Two exceptional scientists, Steven Hawking and our old friend Roger Penrose, addressed the problem and helped to change the course of astronomy. Penrose had been working on the theory of black holes and had made a significant discovery at a time when Hawking had been looking for a suitable project for his PhD thesis. The Einstein gravity equations predicted that if a star was massive enough, it would collapse when it lost its hydrogen fuel into an object so dense that its extreme gravity would prevent even light from escaping its grasp. In other words, it would become totally black—hence the term, *black hole*. Under these conditions, time itself would cease to exist at its border and it would become a hole in space, capable of sucking entire stars into itself.

While astronomers agreed that the equations did predict this result, not too many believed that it reflected reality since the star apparently would have to be a perfectly smooth sphere in order for the black hole to appear. When Penrose addressed this problem, he proved that a star didn't have to be perfectly spherical to collapse to a black hole if it was massive enough. Penrose's equations also indicated that the awesome power of the black hole would result in a singularity. And in 1965 he showed that a mega-star in its end stages could wind up with infinite density. Matter sucked into it would exit the universe forever!

When Hawking read these results, he realized that if he treated the universe like a gigantic star, he could use Penrose's method to work backward to its very beginning. This he did and not only obtained his PhD but also proved that, just like the black hole, the primordial atom of the universe was a singularity, an infinitesimally small point. In effect, the universe was created *ex nihilo*, out of nothing! At least out of nothing that our science can handle. Physics doesn't work within a singularity—it's beyond our physical laws. All we can say is that the universe had a definite beginning, and it seems logical to speculate that it must have been created by an intelligent force; in other words, by a creator!

But Now We have Dark Matter and Dark Energy

As anyone knows who has been paying close attention to the latest developments in astronomy, in the last few decades two discoveries have been made that have thrown astrophysicists into turmoil. Actually, the first was discovered in the 1930's when Fritz Zwicky discovered that the velocity of the galaxies circling within a cluster of galaxies were going too fast to be gravitationally bound to the cluster! The mass of the cluster that could be observed wasn't great enough to hold the cluster together. Therefore, there must be some unseen matter, some *dark matter*, that exists within the cluster. Although the evidence wasn't reliable enough to cause astrophysicists to accept the phenomena as real, in the last couple of decades other phenomena seem to indicate that this dark matter is real and must account for a great deal of the matter in the universe! [17]

In addition to dark matter, in recent years it has been noted that some of the most distant exploding stars are much too faint, suggesting that they are further away than originally thought. In addition, as the galaxies are determined to be farther and farther away from us, they seem to be accelerating and not going away from us at a constant velocity. Since nothing can be observed that would indicate the source for the energy causing this acceleration, it has been called *dark energy* and is supposed to be a part of the space-time continuum itself. Now it is believed that since dark matter must act like particles and be collected in dense regions like galaxies and clusters of galaxies, it must account for only 25% of the unseen matter. Dark energy, on the other hand, must be smoothly distributed throughout space and vary slowly with time. It accounts for the other 75% of the dark components of the universe.

So now we supposedly have a tremendous amount of unseen mass that should be slowing the expansion of the universe, but an even more effective dark energy that's causing it to expand even faster than the original Big-Bang evidence indicated! What's going on?

The answer is that nobody knows. Many solutions for the dark matter have been suggested, but none have satisfactorily explained its nature. For the purposes of our discussion it doesn't really matter what the answer is because all we need to know is that it seems the universe will never contract and become a yo-yo eternal universe. And yet it had a definite beginning.

The Creation of an Accidental Universe

One of the results of Hawking's and Penrose's efforts was that astrophysicists could now determine what happened in the first few seconds, minutes, hours, days, and years after the big bang. It seems that in the beginning, the universe was pure energy at a temperature of thousands of billions of degrees. It was only after a few seconds had passed before it cooled enough for the first building blocks of the subatomic particles were created and many millennia before the first atoms of hydrogen were created.

---

[17] Naturally, it has been speculated that black holes may make up a significant part of this dark matter. However, other evidence indicates that black holes cannot account for more than a small percentage of the apparent mass.

Since the Heisenberg uncertainty principle states that when you consider subatomic particles, you can never precisely determine their position and momentum at the same time, that means that at the beginning of the universe *everything was indeterminate since nothing existed but energy and subatomic particles*! It would have been impossible to predict exactly how the universe was going to develop, and presumably this was just as true for the creator as it would have been for us poor humans if we had been around at the time. All matter, motion, and distribution of quanta was indeterminate in the first energy soup of creation. It is only after the condensation of energy into macroscopic matter that the paths and actions of the material universe could become determinate.

Life in the Universe and the Anthropic Principle

Presumably, it would have been impossible for the creator to determine which galaxy, solar system, planetary system, and planet would create the proper conditions for life to appear. However, there was also presumably little doubt that life would appear *somewhere* within the universe because of its immensity and because of the initial conditions set up for the universe before it was created. This latter has been called the *Anthropic Principle* and involves the values of various universal constants.

In the physical world of science there are a number of universal constants that describe the forces that govern all motion and energy of the stars and planets. In 1961 Robert Dicke, our Princeton astrophysicist who tried to detect the residual radiation from the Big Bang, noted that if certain constants were even slightly different from what we observe, there could be no life in the universe. This had actually been anticipated by Paul Dirac in 1937 when he determined among other facts that stars like our sun could not exist if the gravitational constant were even slightly different. John A. Wheeler, Emeritus Professor of Physics at Princeton and the University of Texas at Austin, proposed that this be called the *Anthropic Principle*, which started the whole modern discussion about the unique, life-designed structure of the universe.[18]

In an article written a few years ago in *Discover* magazine Brad Lemely writes that Martin Rees, Britain's Astronomer Royal, argues in his book, *Just Six Numbers,*

> ...that six numbers underlie the fundamental physical properties of the universe, and that each is the precise value needed to permit life to flourish. As Rees puts it "These six numbers constitute a recipe for the universe." He adds that if any one of the numbers were different

---

[18] To give you some indication of the extent of the interest in this subject, a Google search on the Internet for the Anthropic Principle will yield thousands of quality hits.

"even to the tiniest degree, there would be no stars, no complex elements, no life." [19]

Coming from a scientist, that's a whale of a statement because it implies that the cosmos was designed, which in turn implies a Designer, a creator, of the universe. As Lemely puts it "the numbers uncanny precision has driven some scientists, humbled, into the arms of the theologians." A physicist from the prestigious Massachusetts Institute of Technology, Vera Kistiakowsky, says, "The exquisite order displayed by our scientific understanding of the physical world calls for the divine."

Now of course for any self-respecting determinist this will never do. So Rees has come up with what is actually an old idea derived from quantum mechanics—namely, that this is just one of an infinite number of parallel universes, a *multiverse* [20] in Rees's terminology. Without going into the details, this concept is just one of a number of ideas put forward to retain determinism as a viable option in a universe governed by the Heisenberg uncertainty principle. Since the principle proves that you can never determine the exact position and momentum of a subatomic particle at the same time, this implies that determinism is not valid at the subatomic level. But if you say that whenever there is a chance for more than one future to take place—such as one atom emitting or not emitting a photon—a new universe is created and branches off from this one, then determinism is rescued. Believe it or not, regardless of how wasteful and non-elegant that concept might seem, it is a possible solution of the quantum mechanical equations and is accepted as a viable option by a number of scientists, Rees included. In other words, those who accept the multiple universe idea seem to be taking the advice of Yogi Berra who said, "When you come to a fork in the road, take it!"

Rees puts a different twist on this old argument, however, by proposing "a possibly infinite array of separate big bangs erupted from a primordial dense-matter state." Thus, it isn't surprising that our universe is exquisitely designed for life because we observers couldn't exist in any other type of the infinite variety of universes available. But this begs the issue. If we can't determine how or why a single universe was created in one big bang, why should we exacerbate the problem by positing an infinite number of them? Where did they all come from? And why should such a mind-boggling multiple event ever arise?

Rees is just one of many scientists to propose seemingly off-the-wall hypotheses to explain away the very uncomfortable idea that something intelligent created the universe. Yet, make no mistake, they can't prove any of them through science any more than metaphysicists can prove the existence of the Judaic/Christian God through reason. Even Rees

---

[19] Brad Lemley, "Why is There Life?", *Discover* magazine, November, 2000, p.64.

[20] A term I will *not* use since it is much too contrived and implies a reality impossible to prove.

admits that "The other universes are unavailable to us," although he expresses his hope[21] that proof of some kind is at least theoretically possible. This is *not* science conducted by a scientist as we defined it earlier but speculation by an ordinary person with an axe to grind. At this point all the mathematics in the world won't help him because once you exceed the boundaries of this reality, this space-time continuum, there is no way that you can prove the existence, or non-existence, of anything outside it.

An Unlikely Result of the Multiple-universe Idea

One of the fallouts of the multiple-universe idea that is ignored by many determinists is that if you have an infinite number of parallel universes, then you must accept the idea that there are an infinite number of variations of *you* in existence. This can only be acceptable if you buy into the idea that we don't have free will and that each alternative to a choice we make exists in a parallel universe. That has to be true for all human beings that exist or ever have existed. Then there is no "center of awareness" for any of us because there are an infinite number of them making it impossible to identify one of them as the real "center." The pronoun "I" has lost its meaning. There are no arguments between people that make any sense because in one of those infinite universes you and your opponent have changed sides. There is no morality because while in this universe you may be an upstanding citizen, in another you're an axe murderer. You're not even the person you think of as "you." Figuratively speaking, you're everybody because there will always be a universe in which you are one of an infinite number of types of individuals that can be conceived.

Let's take a simple example. Suppose you look in the cookie jar and see that there is only one cookie left. In one universe you take and eat the cookie, and in a parallel universe you leave the cookie for someone else. Your personality splits at the moment you make your choice. What makes you a cookie-you or a non-cookie-you—why do you remember only one of these actions? According to the multiple universe idea your "I" is split along two different paths even though each "I" is presumably identical in every way. What decides that you should be in the one that you're aware of? Why are you this "I" and not the other "I"? Or even worse, why aren't you both?

Wouldn't it be simpler—and make a lot more sense—to assume that we *selected* the universe we find ourselves in? And if we select one of the possible universes available to us, wouldn't it imply that we brought that universe into being—in a sense that we *created* that universe. After all, the Copenhagen Interpretation says that when we have two different

---

[21] Dare we say "faith?"

possible outcomes, the one we observe becomes "real," like Schrödinger's dead/alive cat. That would mean that all of us are constantly creating the observable universe from those that are available to us. If there are multiple universes, they only exist as *possibilities* with equal chances of becoming real when we make our choices. As I understand it, that is actually closer to the way the quantum equations express our reality than the way most determinists would like to interpret them. They express possibilities, not actualities. And in point of fact I'm in pretty good company because I understand that this is the position that Steven Hawking has taken in relation to the multiple-universe idea.

There is only one way in which I would consider the idea of multiple universes as valid. Someone once pointed out that every person in our world is at the center of his own personal universe. Therefore, when a general says a military operation was successful because he lost only 100 men, he is terribly wrong. What he really lost was 100 centers of the universe!

In Summary

In order for science to work it has to be able to predict future events in the material world, and it has done that with great success. Up through the 19th Century that meant that there were no accidents in the scientific world because everything was determined by natural laws. But in the 20th Century all that changed when scientists discovered that the subatomic world was governed by probabilities not by cause and effect. Free will was possible in a scientific world.

Then there was the problem of creation—was the universe created or was it eternal and infinite? Scientists preferred the latter because it made their job simpler. But then nature dealt them a cruel blow when Hubble discovered the Red Shift and Penzias and Wilson discovered the residual radiation from the Big Bang, confirming the fact that the universe was indeed created billions of years ago. When it was discovered that the universe seemed to be designed specifically to allow life to evolve, the existence of a creator God didn't seem so improbable after all.

Apparently, what we need is a more careful examination of what we now know about the universe by a good philosopher. Some may be surprised to discover that philosophers have often been prescient about matters which are now confronting modern scientists, as we will see in the next chapter.

Chapter 2

The Philosopher's Quest for Knowledge

Ever since the Golden Age of Greece, philosophers have been concerned with epistemology, the study of knowledge. Some started from the premise that we can't rely on what appears to be the real world. For Plato (428-348 B.C.E.) [1] we are like prisoners chained in a cave and forced to look at a screen on which just the shadows of the true objects of reality are projected. In order to create the place where these Ideal Forms could exist, Plato had to invent a new dimension—one which was separate from the world of appearances. Others, such as Aristotle (384-322 B.C.E.) who was a student of Plato, went in the opposite direction and said that there is no world other than the world of our experience. This may be a gross oversimplification of these two monumental philosophies, but it is a broad representation of the two major approaches to the problem of reality that philosophers have taken ever since. The former group equates reality with the ideas of the mind, with idealism. The latter equates it with the physical world, with materialism and the physical universe.

This dichotomy became most pronounced in the 17th and 18th centuries with the Modern Philosophers and the start of modern science. When the Copernican revolution stood the world of thought on its head, it seemed that almost everything that mankind had thought about the universe was wrong. We weren't on a flat, rectangular stage[2] with the great heavenly spheres rotating about us, but on a little ball of water and dirt spinning around a star just like the other planets. It wasn't just the Church that was knocked off its pins by this concept but the men who thought about the nature of thought, itself.

Sir Francis Bacon isolated the problem when he stated that the only way we could learn anything about the cosmos was through inductive reasoning, not by making *a priori* assumptions and then "proving" solutions through deductive reasoning, alone. That meant that the quest for certainty that was so dear to the hearts of all metaphysicists had to be modified.

---

[1] We will use the recent practice of identifying the period before year zero with B.C.E ,Before the Common Era., and the period after as C.E., the Common Era.

[2] That's where the expression, "from the four corners of the earth," comes from. Indeed, our culture is immersed in such phrases: "He traveled to the ends of the earth," the sun "sets" and the moon "rises," the stars "whirl" around us, suggesting that the old cosmology is still very much with us.

The Deceiving Search for Certainty

Mathematical reasoning is deductive, and its definite, undeniably true conclusions from seemingly self-evident axioms are hugely attractive. However, it is essential that a premise be universally true for the conclusion to be universally true. "All men have two legs...Socrates is a man...therefore, Socrates has two legs" may be true for Socrates but not for Pegleg Pete. That's what the logicians call a valid, unsound argument. It's valid because it follows the laws of logic, but it's unsound because the premise is wrong! The problem is to get universally true premises, and if you are in the pursuit of certainty, you can't rely on premises of observed repeated phenomena because you can't afford to spend eternity making sure that the phenomena never change. Since mathematics was built on seemingly pure *a priori* rational axioms which were independent from observations of the physical world, it appeared that the same type of reasoning could be used to discover the truths about reality. All you needed were some undeniably true ideas which already existed in the minds of every human in order to build valid conclusions through deductive reasoning.

Bacon's genius was to say that the philosophers had lost sight of the way humans think. We think inductively. That means that when certain phenomena repeat consistently, we make the assumption (i.e., we *induce*) that they will continue to do so in the foreseeable future. We couldn't successfully conduct our lives if we didn't. The sun will continue to come up in the east and set in the west; the four seasons will repeat year after year so that the time to plant and the time to reap won't change significantly; the position of the moon and the sun will affect the tides in the same way, month after month, so the fishermen know when and where to cast their nets.[3]

It was Bacon's contention that it was time for the philosophers to forget their passion for certainty and get back to the practical way we all determine the truth about the natural world. Gather as much data as you can to be reasonably sure through inductive reasoning that your suppositions are reliable and then deduce your conclusions from these. The resulting theories may only be certain as long as they aren't altered or disproved by further evidence, but in the meantime you can start to build a reasonably firm foundation of knowledge about the physical world. In other words, the materialists' approach was the right one to take if you wanted to make any practical progress in science. And indeed we have.

But in the milieu of the 17th and 18th centuries when the world of the philosophers had been turned upside down by the Copernican/Galilean revelations, the idealists weren't about to put down their scepter without a fight. And one of the first to take on the challenge in a significant way was

---

[3] And of course the old inductive adages gleaned from years of experience: never trust a politician who says, "I give you my word," nor a debtor who says, "The check is in the mail."

Descartes, who in his own right had also made significant contributions to science and mathematics.

Descartes' *Cogito Ergo Sum* Proof and the Cartesian Circle

The Copernican revolution that the earth was not the center of the universe implied that the previous age's *a priori* assumptions had been wrong and that anything derived from them was also wrong. In order to avoid this error, Descartes vowed to eliminate any prior assumptions that could not be proven to be correct. And in so doing, he wound up eliminating everything, including external reality, itself!

Now it should be made clear at the outset that although Descartes went to this extreme extent to form the foundation for his metaphysics, the one thing he did not eliminate from his assumptions was the existence of God—indeed, his whole thesis hinges on positing an evil God intent upon deceiving him. He says suppose that all that he thinks is real is merely an illusion created by this evil Being. Well, even though that might be true, the one thing that the deceptive God can't change is the fact that Descartes can and does think about the deception—indeed, the evil God's only purpose for making a deceptive world is to confound Descartes' reasoning powers. Thus, Descartes comes to the conclusion that he can't think without existing—*cogito ergo sum*, "I think, therefore I am."

No one, before or since, has come up with a more basic premise on which to build a philosophy on the nature of reality. On this very simple expression a whole series of philosophies have been created because, as we shall see later on, it implies that mind and body are two separate substances. And that would make free will possible in a deterministic world.

There are problems with it, however, because it also requires a proof of God's existence and an assumption that this particular God is not evil but benevolent and wouldn't create a world designed to deceive.

In the process of creating his *cogito* proof Descartes states that he will only accept ideas which are "clearly and distinctly true." It would appear that he initially accepts the *cogito* as one of these ideas, but later on he claims that no idea can be metaphysically clear and distinct if there is no benevolent God to back it up. Thus he is forced to develop a proof of God's existence. The validity of what has become known as an *ontological proof* will be discussed later; all we need do here is to note that Descartes says that this proof is essential to his clear and distinctly true ideas.

As a number of his contemporaries pointed out, Descartes has employed circular reasoning here because he can only prove the existence of God if he clearly and distinctly perceives the truth of his proof. But he can't clearly and distinctly perceive that his proof is true until after he proves that God exists. The validity of *cogito ergo sum* therefore can't be clearly and distinctly perceived.

This has become known as the *Cartesian circle*, and it has occupied the attention of a number of philosophers who have tried to reinterpret Descartes' basic assumptions to get rid of the circularity. None, including Descartes himself, has been very successful. However, if one eliminates the necessity for *metaphysical certainty* and is willing to accept the notion of *practical probability*, then there is no need to assume the world is controlled by a benevolent God or generate a questionable proof for His existence.[4]

In our modern world we are quite familiar with the possibility of someone deceiving us with a false version of reality. The famous 1930's radio broadcast by Orson Wells that simulated an attack on Earth by Martians is an excellent case in point. Thousands of listeners were convinced that our world was under attack by extra-terrestrial beings. In this case, Orson Wells assumed the character of Descartes' evil God by creating a reality that was completely false, but was accepted as the truth by people all over the country. A later 60's TV program, *Mission Impossible*, created weekly programs in which a super-talented team of experts created deceiving scenarios to convince the bad guys that it was safe to divulge their guilt, or reveal where their loot was stashed, or persuade them that their associates were trying to cheat them.

But an even more compelling example can be found in the recent development of virtual reality with modern computers. People wearing a special helmet with tiny internal PC monitors can look at a world entirely created by a computer which changes the visual scene according to the head movements sensed by the motion detectors built into the helmet. In the not too distant future it is conceivable that an entire body suit could be made that would be so completely controlled by a super computer that the person wearing it would be unable to distinguish the computer-generated world from the real one.

What is needed is a physical reason to doubt the reality of the external world without resorting to an external agent intent on deception. We can use the recent movie adaptation of Sylvia Nasar's book, *A Beautiful Mind*, as a possible scenario for examining this question.

The Schizophrenia of John Nash and his Remission

John Nash is a mathematical genius and Nobel Laureate in economics who contracted schizophrenia in his 30's after making significant contributions in "games of strategy, economic rivalry, computer architecture, the shape of the universe, the geometry of imaginary spaces, [and] the mystery of prime numbers."[5] However, for the next three decades

---

[4] If you're wondering why we should bother to go to all the trouble, I think it will become clear later on when we consider mind/body dualism.

[5] Sylvia Nasar, *A Beautiful Mind*, A Touchstone Book Published by Simon & Schuster, New York, 2001, p. 12.

he was lost to the world of mathematics, and indeed to the world, itself, and wandered in a never, never land of delusion and misery. Through the love and concern of his wife Alicia and his colleagues, and as Nash himself put it, through the natural process of aging, he attained a remarkable and at the time very rare remission that appears to be permanent. It is only a matter of speculation but it is not unreasonable to assume that part of his recovery was his intellectual ability to discern illusion from reality and make a conscious decision to reject the former in preference for the latter.

The movie that was made from Sylvia Nasar's wonderful book is not a true adaptation of the biography, but as Nasar put it herself in a televised talk, it was never intended to be. However, it still reflects the spirit of the genius, illness, lost years, and recovery in a dynamic and essentially faithful representation of the life of this remarkable man.

We will refer to the movie rather than the book since it is a much more forceful and clear-cut story of delusion and recovery than the book, which is understandably quite complex and pertains to matters which are not necessary for our purposes.

A Redefinition of the Cartesian Proof

Let us suppose that John Nash is at the point where he realizes that the people and events that he has been seeing are delusional. He doesn't need to postulate an evil God because he already has one in his brain called schizophrenia, and it really is trying to deceive him. Therefore, he can't trust his senses to tell him the truth but must find some other way of differentiating between reality and illusion.

Even Descartes in the sixth *Meditation* mentions the doubts he had had in his senses—that visions at a distance were not the same close up, that all sensations he had when awake he could also have when asleep, and that he "saw nothing to rule out the possibility that my natural constitution made me prone to error even in matters which seemed to me most true."[6] To Nash these same doubts were not just the result of speculation but of real experience.

In our movie scenario Nash believes that he has been hired by the National Security Agency to weed out Soviet spies by deciphering hidden codes in magazines and newspapers. It is not until his wife shows him the "classified" documents he thought he had been mailing to his "control," which had actually been collecting dust in an old abandoned mail box, that he realizes that his elaborate spy work with the NSA is an illusion. How then can he rely on the truth of any idea he has or anything he sees.

In his case, he can't get rid of the illusions by proving a benevolent God exists, but rather by applying the logic of his reasoning powers to sort out the real from the false. For example, he finds out that the niece of his

---

[6] *The Philosophical Writings of Descartes*, Volume II, translated by John Cottingham, Robert Stoothoff, and Dugald Murdoch; Cambridge University Press, 1984, p. 53..

best friend is an illusion when he realizes that she never grows old. And if that's the case, his so-called best friend is also an illusion because he was the one that introduced his niece to Nash. He already knows his NSA "control" is an illusion because he was the one who told him to deposit his decoded material in that abandoned mail box.

Later when his illness is largely in remission and he's back to teaching, he's approached by a member of the Nobel Prize committee whom he has never met. He immediately stops one of his students and asks, "Do you see him." When she says yes, he tells the man, "You'll have to forgive me, but I'm very suspicious of new people." Once he comes to his clear and distinct method of distinguishing real people from illusionary ones, he's able to operate rationally in the real world, even though he's still aware of the fake ones.

One of the things that was to Nash's advantage was that science had proven that nature was rational. We can investigate the world around us through logic. That means that if there is a God, we know that He is not deceptive because the non-deceptive nature of the universe has been proven time and time again in the last four centuries. There is no longer a need to prove God's existence or even to consider whether or not He or She exists.

Thus, Nash obtains a practical certainty about what is real and what is not. It is a certainty that allows him to function in the real world, resume his teaching, and once more attack the more difficult problems in the world of mathematics. But the problem still remains—is this a metaphysical certainty in the way that Descartes would define it? If it isn't, can this method of proving *cogito ergo sum* lead to clear and distinct ideas about the real world?

Does this Technique Break the Cartesian Circle?

As we've noted, it is an apparent universal desire among humans to hang their hats on something that they can believe is absolutely certain. But as someone said to Nash, "the only thing that I am absolutely certain about is that there is no such thing as certainty." Most people think that scientific knowledge is certain, but as Popper[7] points out, a scientific theory is correct only as long as it isn't proven to be false. I would put it in a less extreme way by saying that a scientific theory has a high probability of truth until contrary evidence or logic reduces that probability to a point where it can no longer be accepted.

But let's take a look at what can happen to metaphysical certainties. A second before any intelligent 17th century person understood the logic of the Copernican/Galilean heliocentric universe, they would possess a clear and distinct idea that the sun, moon, and stars circled the

---

[7] Karl Popper (1902-1994) held that a theory can only be acceptable if its falsification is possible, and the falsification of a theory can be certain only where unqualified proof is impossible.

earth. A few seconds later they presumably would not. A clear and distinct idea that could easily be defined by Descartes' method as metaphysically certain was demolished in the blink of an eye. And it should be clearly stated that the certainty was demolished by inductive/deductive scientific reasoning based on physically observable facts, not by a metaphysical method which supposedly would lead to certainty. Clear and distinct ideas which have been held by millions over the years have been demolished by new discoveries countless times. We must use some other criterion to decide which ideas have the best probability of being true.

Mind/Body Dualism

Descartes' *cogito* led to what has become known as mind/body dualism, or Cartesian dualism. In effect Descartes was saying that he could doubt the real existence of his body, but he could not doubt the existence of his mind, because in the very act of doubting he realizes that he is using his mind. Therefore, the mind itself must be a separate entity from the body. But if this is the case, how can the two entities, mind and body, interact? For Descartes the point of contact between the soul and the body was the pineal gland because it appeared to be the only organ in the brain that was not bilaterally duplicated. But that begs the issue. The problem isn't where the contact is made, but how it could be possible that two completely different *substances*,[8] the material body and the transcendent mind, could interact at all.

It has been said that subsequent philosophy, especially by the 17th and 18th century Modern Philosophers, was an attempt to escape this Cartesian impasse. For Malebranche (1638-1715) the dichotomy could be resolved by what came to be known as *occasionalism*. God is the only true cause of anything, nothing in the mind can influence the body and vice versa, and when someone moved his or her finger, it was only on that *occasion* that God caused the finger to move.[9] Spinoza (1632-1677) took this to its perhaps more obvious conclusion and said that everything was God, there was only one true *substance*, and nothing caused anything else to happen that wasn't predetermined by God. Thus for him the mental and physical were simply different aspects of the same *substance*. Leibniz (1646-1716) came along and in effect said, "No, no, you've got it all wrong. What's happening is parallelism between the pre-established harmony between soul and body. Mind does not influence body, nor does body influence mind since that interaction is impossible. Instead, God set them off in perfect synchronicity when He created them at the beginning of time." Determinism raises its anti-intellectual head once more, and we

---

[8] The reason why this ancient philosophical term results in the problems with Cartesian dualism will be discussed later on.
[9] This not only posits a ridiculously busy God but it also makes one wonder why He would bother!

don't have to worry about anything we do or think since it's all been predetermined anyway. [10]

It should be noted that each of these philosophies represents an attempt to solve the Cartesian dualism of mind and body. To a practical layman the results are not persuasive. We conduct our lives assuming with great justification that our thoughts control our actions and that it makes a difference, morally and intellectually, how we conduct our relationships with each other and with our society. And yet the remarkable thing is that the ideas by these philosophers that thought and action are not connected have survived for centuries and are regarded by many with respect and something approaching awe even though these same people conduct their lives as if there isn't one scintilla of truth to them.

Bishop Berkeley's Immaterialism

As we said above, some Modern Philosophers like Spinoza recognized these problems and avoided them by denying any distinction at all between mind and body. Another, Bishop George Berkeley (1685-1753), solved the mind/body dichotomy by claiming that all external reality is illusion. Body (i.e., the material world) then becomes merely the perception of mind.

Berkeley published his *Principles of Human Knowledge* in 1710. His approach took Malebranche's occasionalism to a logical extreme that differed from Spinoza's by maintaining that material objects were only ideas that existed in the minds of finite human spirits as well as the infinite spirit we call God. Berkeley felt that by destroying the "illusion" of material *substance* through his concept of *immaterialism*, he effectively removed the materialist's basis for atheism. Naturally, once all material bodies are conceived as mere ideas, Descartes' mind/body dichotomy is eliminated.

It's intriguing to realize that if you decide to accept the basic premise of Berkeley's immaterialism that all material objects are merely ideas in our minds, you have to accept the existence of God since there is no other way to account for the stability of the external world without the object-creating mind of that omnipotent being. He points out that he has no control over what he sees when he opens his eyes, so there must be some other agent that creates a stable world, and of course that agent or spirit is called God. This is necessary since there is no other way to account for the fact that objects in the external world remain even when we are not observing them. Of course this "proof" of God's existence has no more persuasive force than the more traditional ontological and cosmological proofs which we will discuss later on, but it is an interesting variation none

---

[10] If all things including thoughts are determined by natural forces, then we can't praise a man as a genius for his wonderful thoughts any more than we can congratulate a stick of wood for landing in a field of water lilies while floating downstream. Determinism makes the personal attribute of intelligence meaningless and without merit.

the less. However, the real question remains—does immaterialism resolve mind/body dualism?

The answer is yes, of course it does, but can we really accept the idea that all material substance is just an idea in our minds and in the mind of God? Most of Berkeley's contemporaries didn't think so and in fact rejected his entire thesis out of hand, as no doubt most people in our contemporary world would. But recently some philosophers have been taking another look at immaterialism, probably in light of the discoveries mentioned in the previous chapter. If the nature of the material world depends on the way we observe it as the Copenhagen interpretation and the Heisenberg uncertainty principle claim, then Berkeley's immaterialism has actually acquired some support from modern scientific theory.

In addition, there is some surprising support for the theory that can be derived from the thoughts of a fourth-century bishop who made a brilliant analysis of the nature of time.

St. Augustine's Ideas about Time Past and Time Future

In Book XI of his *Confessions* Augustine makes a very thorough analysis of time, pointing out that the only time that is "real" is the present. What has happened in the past does not exist anywhere except in our memories, and that which is to come is not yet real. He says, "If future and past events exist, I want to know where they are…"

This is actually an excellent attempt to describe a multidimensional universe at a time when such a concept was unheard of. To describe the "where" of the past and the future, we have to examine what is meant by a fourth dimension. Mathematicians describe one dimension as a line, two dimensions as a plane, and three dimensions as space. The latter two of these can be represented mathematically by coordinates[11] or axes which are perpendicular to each other, as shown in the following diagrams.

Two Dimensions   *Three Dimensions*

These two Cartesian diagrams seem quite natural since they exist in our world, but a fourth dimension is impossible to represent in this type of diagram because it would require a fourth line to be drawn at right angles

---

[11] Usually called Cartesian coordinates in honor of their inventor, Descartes.

to all three axes of the three-dimensional diagram simultaneously, an impossibility in three-dimensional space. However, we are actually experiencing a four-dimensional world because we "travel" through time. We experience time as a flow of events, an intimate part of our existence. In this sense we are four-dimensional beings because we couldn't even act without the fourth dimension of time.

Perhaps an easier way of comprehending this is to consider how we see our three-dimensional world.. There's left and right, up and down, in front and behind. But even though we think of time as flowing, we couldn't say that it is flowing in only one of these directions since all these directions are moving with us through time at the same rate. Therefore, time must flow in a direction that's along all three directions at once. And since our space is three-dimensional, we must assume that time constitutes a fourth dimension.

As Einstein implied, we are definitely part and parcel of the space-time continuum.

But once you consider the creation event of the Big Bang, you have to consider the possibility of an additional timeless dimension. Time started with creation. Therefore, something outside of our space-time must have created it. In the past we have called this something God and described Him as *transcendent*. Using the Cartesian terminology described above we can call the transcendent dimension the *fifth* dimension.

To get some idea of the fifth dimension, imagine that two-dimensional beings exist on a plane. For them time would be their third dimension. If we passed a billiard ball through their two-dimensional world,

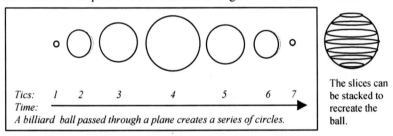

Tics: 1   2   3   4   5   6   7
Time: ⟶

A billiard ball passed through a plane creates a series of circles.

The slices can be stacked to recreate the ball.

it would seem to the inhabitants as if a series of circles suddenly appeared, starting as a point, expanding to the circumference of the ball, and then diminishing to a point before vanishing.

The same thing would happen to us if a fifth-dimensional super being somehow passed a fifth-dimensional ball through our space, except we would experience it as a sequence of three-dimensional spheres. Just as we could take the series of circular slices of our billiard ball as it appeared to our two-dimensional friends and stack them up to recreate an image of our three-dimensional ball, so could the super being recreate his four-dimensional ball from the series of three-dimensional spherical "slices" which appeared in our space. Make no mistake, each ball that would appear in its own "tic" of time would be complete and individually separate from all the other balls that appeared in their "tics" of time. But the super being

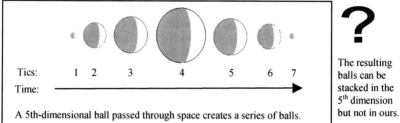

Tics: 1 2 3 4 5 6 7

Time:

A 5th-dimensional ball passed through space creates a series of balls.

The resulting balls can be stacked in the 5th dimension but not in ours.

would see them all as parts of a complete entity.

It should be emphasized that *all* the objects in our universe exist in four dimensions—people, furniture, houses, world, solar system, milky way, and all the galaxies are traveling through the fourth dimension—i.e., they all pass through the "present" at the same rate. And indeed our super friend would comprehend our universe from his five-dimensional perspective as our past, present, and future all contained in one four-dimensional creation.

Now consider what we view as our past. In a sense, we can comprehend our past as an eternally fixed series of events, even though our past actions were the result of free choices, freely made. In other words, we can imagine the way our super being sees it, as an unchanging complete whole. But in the tics of time that are so rapidly created in our world and just as rapidly disappear, we exercise our free will while creating an instantly determined past.

For example, when a news anchor on live TV asks a question of a reporter in China, the reporter stands there for a few seconds before he or she answers. In fact, they answer as soon as they hear the question because it takes a few seconds for the question to reach them and the same time for their words and image to come back to us. In other words, we are looking into the past to an event that has already happened..

That's actually the way we see everything If we consider the way we see the external world, even when it is only inches away from our eyes, it is by the light reflected off the objects in the world. While light travels at an incredible speed, it still takes a finite time for it to reach us, even though in many cases that's less than a fraction of a nanosecond. Therefore, everything that we see about us exists in the past, no matter how immediate that past might seem. Even our sense of touch reaches into the past because the touch signal travels through nerves to our center of awareness at actually less than the speed of light. That means our bodies also exist for us only in the past with all its emotions, feelings, pain, and ecstasy. We are quite literally surrounded by a past that exists for us only in our minds.

That's the way that God can see our four dimensional world *in toto* and know everything that is going to happen *in our future* even though we are still exercising our free will *in our present*. Therefore, even if God knows our future, He sees it as one that we freely made, thus preserving His omniscience and permitting our use of free will at the same time.

Now consider this in the light of Berkeley's immaterialism. We are figuratively riding on the knife edge between time-future and time-past. All that has occurred in the past is not present for us *except in our minds*. Despite the fact that we may have a record in books and on tape, as well as the evidence of any changes we have made in our environment, none of this literally reconstructs the past—for us four-dimensional beings that has disappeared forever.

Even if we try to consider objects and events occurring in the present, it is really only the memory of each object and event that stays in our minds. The chair that we see at "tic" one of time is really not the same as the chair we see at "tic" two. Even if only one electron changed position, one cell sloughed off, one molecule altered, one microbe added or subtracted, they are no longer the same. And mathematically they only exist on the fourth axis at two different "time-positions," still in all their three-dimensional glory but separated from each other by one "tic" of time. Our mental observation of chair-present exists for a fleeting moment before it becomes chair-past and something that we can only access in our minds. In addition, chair-future is not available to us, but only as something that we *expect* until it comes along the time line into our comprehension. In other words, both chair-future and chair-past are nothing more than ideas—you might say they are Berkeley ideas.

But what about chair-present? Even though it is destined to become chair-past, doesn't it *really* exist, riding with us on our knife edge of the present? If it too is simply a Berkeley idea, then we would have to say our bodies are also Berkeley ideas. But ideas that reside where? Certainly not in another idea called the brain. And if chair-present isn't a Berkeley idea but a material thing that exists only for a blink, how does a material brain that also exists for only a blink comprehend it? Something must tie those physical brain blinks together to form a mental thought!

In fact, the only thing that does not exist in the past for us is our minds! Descartes' and Berkeley's concepts that the mind is a non-physical *substance*—perhaps best identified as a transcendent *substance*—begins to look more and more interesting.

How did Other Philosophers Approach Mind/Body Dualism?

John Locke (1632-1704) avoided the problem of the dichotomy by essentially ignoring it. For him all knowledge comes through the senses, impinging on the brain which starts out as a "blank slate," a *tabula rasa*. That seemed eminently sensible until Kant pointed out that if the brain was truly a blank slate, it would be incapable of organizing the information it received and would just retain it as a jumble of incomprehensible facts. So mind must indeed bring something to the table in the way that it organizes and analyzes the sense information it receives. But where does mind come from?

For materialists like Julien Offray de la Mettrie (1709-1751) the living being was a purposive, automatic, dynamic machine which created its own mind from physical *substance*. There was no dichotomy of mind and body because all was body, the opposite of the Berkeley proposition that all was mind. Subsequent materialists pointed to the brain as the specially designed organ which produced mind, just as the stomach and intestines were designed to operate the digestion. And at this point it is essential for us to consider the philosophy of the one many consider to be the greatest materialist of them all—David Hume.

The *Dialogues* of David Hume

In 1777 the *Dialogues* of David Hume (1711-1776) were published posthumously and along with his previously published philosophical treatises became a standard to judge all subsequent considerations of materialism. The three protagonists whom Hume creates to conduct the dialogues represent three conflicting points of view: *Demeas* represents the orthodox Christian theology of the 18th century; *Cleanthes* professes a belief in a creator whose design can be detected in the material world—in other words, he takes the point of view of the popular 18th Century version of Natural Theology—and *Philo* is the adversary. and the spokesperson for Hume, himself, who points out the fallacies of both views and proposes his conception of materialism. One of the more striking things about Hume's presentation is that these three protagonists represent the kind of internal conversation that many of us have conducted in our own minds when we've puzzled over the questions of God and life. Those of us brought up in a Christian environment recognize in *Demeas* the convictions of our youth, even though those may have been severely modified if not eliminated in later years. *Cleanthes* represents the attempt to reconcile the conflict between the spiritual and the material. And of course *Philo* is very much with us in this scientific, materialistic age.

Although *Demeas* is used in the beginning to set the stage for the development of Hume's arguments, he is not really a major factor in the discussion that follows. *Cleanthes* outlines the major argument for the *Dialogues* by comparing the operation of the world to a great machine, composed of an infinite number of lesser machines. And just as we can look at one of our machines and realize that it had to be designed by someone with intelligence, so can we consider the universe as a design by an "Author of Nature" whose intelligence is analogous to mankind's—in other words, God and humans think alike.

Philo refutes this argument by saying that if you're going to rely on a proof by analogy, you must make certain that the cases are *exactly* similar, a condition that is impossible to establish here. Even in the case of human-designed machines, one cannot determine the intelligence of the person who built, say, a yacht because it could have been done by a mental defective who was simply following a plan. To put it in more materialistic form he says:

> ... For ought we can know a priori, matter may contain the source or spring of order originally within itself as well as mind does; and there is no more difficulty in conceiving, that the several elements, from an internal unknown cause, may fall into the most exquisite arrangement [12]

...thus anticipating Darwin's natural selection by over 100 years. But since there wasn't any mechanism in the 18th century to account for such an "internal unknown cause," Hume had to have *Philo* continue to create other arguments for many more pages to lend more weight to his refutation of the argument from design. It makes one think that if Hume had lived after the 1859 publication of Darwin's *Origin of Species*, he might not have thought it necessary to even write the *Dialogues*. The mechanically automatic nature of evolution would seem to be the answer to a materialist's prayers and devastating to any argument from design.

However, there are aspects of the theory of evolution that might be used to support *Cleanthes'* position. For example, in the 18th century it was possible for *Philo* to say the following:

> But, allowing that we were to take the operations of one part of nature upon another, for the foundation of our judgment concerning the origin of the whole, (which never can be admitted,) yet why select so minute, so weak, so bounded a principle, as the reason and design of animals is found to be upon this planet? What peculiar privilege has this little agitation of the brain which we call thought, that we must thus make it the model of the whole universe? ...
>
> ... Is there any reasonable ground to conclude, that the inhabitants of other planets possess thought, intelligence, reason, or any thing similar to these faculties in men? ... can we imagine that she incessantly copies herself throughout so immense a universe? [13]

---

[12] *David Hume; Dialogues Concerning Natural Religion*; http://www.anselm.edu/ homepage/dbanach/dnr.htm. Copyright © 2006 David Banach, [146].
[13] Ibid, [148].

Now, there is indeed "reasonable ground" to suspect that our intelligence will be duplicated in other life forms because of that same theory which seems to support the materialist's position—Darwin's theory of evolution. If evolution produced a brand of rationality in us, and indeed in all the creatures in the animal kingdom, it worked as well as it did because it reflected the rational character of nature, itself. And because of the success of Newton's and Einstein's formulations in predicting the motion of the stars and planets throughout the observable universe, there is every reason to believe that evolution will duplicate such a successful adaptation wherever it finds life. Our success in discovering the laws of nature would not be possible unless our intelligence reflected the logical design of the material cosmos.

But the big question that *Cleanthes* never really addressed in Hume's discourse is "Design for what purpose?" The overwhelming evidence indicates that species are not and never have been immutable. So there can be no validity to the argument that the marvelous efficiency of plants and animals in their environments were the result of God's designing skills when he "made" them and plopped them on Earth. This is what the *Cleanthes* of Hume's time believed. Hume was quite right in pointing out the fallacies of such a belief. So the purpose of any intentional design is not just to make things operate optimally in a static world.

But if we ignore individual "designs" and concentrate on the possibility of a general "purpose" for the universe, then *Philo's* arguments no longer apply. But then neither do *Cleanthes'*. As we will see in a later section of this chapter, St. Thomas' fifth argument claiming that the purpose that we see all around us indicates an original Designer was for Immanuel Kant the most persuasive of them all and could not be easily disproved.

So What can We Conclude?

There are lots of reasons for supposing that the mind is a different entity from the body, even if we admit that determinism is present in the material world. There is no doubt that the science of material bodies is repeatable and universal—it can be used to predict events not only here on earth but in the stars, planets, and galaxies of the universe as well. The physicists and chemists are being quite reasonable when they push so hard for determinism because in the world that they study they must rely on it to prove the validity or invalidity of their theories. If there was no material determinism, science could not predict future events, and indeed could not be used to determine the natural laws of the universe.

But by the same token, most of us are convinced that we can change the outcome of material events by physically acting on our thoughts. When a pool player hits the eight ball towards the side pocket, we can easily prevent it from dropping in by grabbing it first. Its destiny has been changed by a thought. If we believe that this action was inspired by a free-willed though whimsical thought, then there is no way that the mind that produced the thought could be a part of the physical, material, deterministic world.

It brings us back to Francis Bacon and his insistence on accepting inductive reasoning as the only practical way to understand how we think. We can't *prove* that our thoughts can be free and not determined, but we operate in practice as if they are. We believe that we make decisions which affect our lives and the lives of others. As I've said, we couldn't operate in this world if we didn't. I would much rather join with Bacon and say that instead of searching for certainty in this uncertain world we should accept that which in a practical sense seems evident to us all. Just as in Bacon's opinion the common man *knew* through inductive reasoning that the seasons and tides were repeatable, we *know* that our thoughts govern our actions and that we have free will.

But can two Completely Different Substances interact?

For the 17th and 18th century philosophers, this was the question that they couldn't get around without creating the drastic and largely unbelievable solutions we've seen. Their problem actually lay in their use of the term *substance* which is a holdover from the ancient philosophical attempts to understand reality. *Substance* was thought to be the underlying solid "stuff" of material reality as opposed to its attributes. The latter could change—like a green apple compared to a red one—but the underlying substrate was unalterable. By the time of Descartes, primary *substance* was divided into material *substance* for the physical world and spiritual *substance* for the non-material world. Thus by believing in their own definitions and that they were unrelated entities, philosophers were faced with the problem of describing how the two could interact with each other, if indeed any interaction at all was possible.

We are not faced with this difficulty since the entire ancient concept of *substance* has no meaning in the modern scientific world. We now know that there is nothing "solid" about the material world—it is simply an illusion created by the binding forces of atoms largely comprised of empty space and best represented in quantum mechanics by standing waves of energy. If therefore there is no material *substance* in the ancient philosophical sense, then spiritual *substance* is just as undefined—we don't really know what it is anymore than we really know what the material "stuff" of the universe is outside our mathematical descriptions of it. And there is nothing to prevent us from assuming from our practical experience that we, as transcendent non-determinant entities, can apparently direct the actions of material bodies without describing how that interaction can take place.

But if spiritual *substance* is undefined, the question now becomes, is it possible to prove the existence of a spiritual God metaphysically as the philosopher-theologians attempted to do in Medieval times? Can we use our reasoning powers to go either from our innate ideas or from our observation of the world around us to a proof that God exists and that He created a purposeful universe?

The Medieval Attempt to Prove the Existence of God

We've seen how philosophers approach the problem of epistemology, the study of knowledge. Is there any possibility that they can use whatever they think they have discovered to create a definitive proof of God's existence? A number have tried over the centuries, but their success rate leaves something to be desired.

St. Anselm of Canterbury (1033-1109)—*The Ontological Argument*

When medieval theologians came to know the Greek philosophers, especially Plato and Aristotle, they thought they saw a way to prove the existence of God through reason alone. It is characteristic of human beings to bring certain preconceptions about reality to any argument, especially one concerning the nature of reality, itself. This is especially true of the theologians and philosophers we will be considering here. In the case of St. Anselm, his argument is predicated on the concept of God as a being who is greater than anything else in existence. If we accept that definition, then according to Anselm God is "a being than which nothing greater can be conceived." The argument goes that since even a fool can understand the concept of something that is greater than anything he can imagine, that something must exist in reality, because if it didn't, there would be something greater than what he has in his understanding, making that which he has in his understanding not the greatest thing that can be imagined. This has been labeled by Immanuel Kant as the ontological argument, one which is based on the nature of being, itself.

Unfortunately, it is also a tautological argument—i.e., a circular argument—that proves what it originally assumes, namely that something that is greater than anything we humans can imagine is called God, defined as an omnipotent, omniscient, monolithic creator. That's an assumption we have no way of proving. For all we know, the universe was created by a committee. Furthermore, we have no *a priori* proof that God is omnipotent and omniscient. We're just assuming that He/She/It is because we can't conceive of a being who could create the universe that wasn't all-powerful and all-knowing.

It also depends on a particular definition of what a "greater" reality is. According to Anselm, that which exists in *reality* is greater than that which exists only in the mind. There is no *a priori* or innate reason to believe this. What we know about the external world, as we have shown, comes to us only through our senses as these signals impinge themselves on our brains. Even though there are things "out there" that can affect our bodies and even cause our bodies to cease functioning, there is no imperative criteria that those things are "greater" than our minds—minds which in their own right might be transcendent.

In addition, we know that what exists in our minds does not necessarily exist in the material world. But if we are talking about a transcendent God, He wouldn't exist in the material world in any case. So talking about God existing in *reality* is talking about something that doesn't exist in the material world. Before Anselm can talk about a reality we can't examine and measure, he has to first establish the idea that such a reality exists and that God resides there, a concept which Anselm would be hard put to address, let alone prove.

It is also an argument that leaves one with a feeling of unease. Even if one were willing to accept the existence of an all-powerful God, this rather specious reasoning of St. Anselm's is unconvincing to most of us as a definitive proof of His existence (and in particular to Immanuel Kant, as we shall see).

St. Thomas Aquinas (1225-1274)—*The Cosmological & Teleological Arguments*

Aquinas came to his proofs with two major preconceptions: he believed that the nature of God was identical to the Christian God, and that God's existence could and should be proven from empirical evidence rather than from pure reason. In other words, his proofs are intended to be *a posteriori*, after the fact, not *a priori*, before the fact, as the ontological arguments are.

The first proof is the argument from motion. All things that we see that are in motion have been set in motion by something else. Since all moving objects are governed by this "law," none can be both mover and moved. Therefore, there must be a first mover, or Prime Mover (Aristotle's term), and "this everyone understands to be God."

The second proof is from *efficient causes*—i.e., causes that result in a specific effect. Nowhere in nature do we find anything which is the efficient cause of itself. So once again, we can't infinitely regress through efficient causes, but must logically come upon a first efficient cause, and once again give it the name of God.

The third proof is particularly interesting in the light of modern science because it is essentially equivalent to the entropy principle. The latter states that all things in nature "run down," that energy always flows from a greater energy to a lesser in a closed system. In the 13th century there was no formal concept of energy in the modern scientific sense, so Aquinas described it as the argument from "possibility and necessity." This was actually an astute observation that all things go from the possible to the actual (or as physicists say, from the *potential* to the *kinetic*) and that eventually these things can "be corrupted, and consequently, it is possible for them to...not be." When they are in that non-being state, they cannot make something else come into existence—they have no potential. Aquinas then goes on to state that since something material can't come out of nothing, we must come to the conclusion that there exists a being "having of itself its own necessity, and not receiving it from another, but rather causing in others their necessity." And once again, Aquinas claims that "all men speak of [this being] as God."

Aquinas' fourth proof is from gradation—some things are better than others, stronger, wiser, truer, etc. And of course this gradation of all good things must find its ultimate expression in the perfection of that which "we call God." Or at least that which Aquinas *defines* as God, completing the tautological circle once again.

The final proof is for many the most persuasive, although it was quickly mocked by Aquinas' contemporaries. That is the argument from design—the *teleological* argument. All natural bodies seem to act as though "to obtain the best result." In other words, it seems as if there was a purpose to the design of the cosmos. Since no design can occur spontaneously without being created by someone with knowledge and intelligence, we have to posit an "intelligent being by whom all natural things are directed to their end; and this being we call God."

Many years later Voltaire parodied this argument in *Candide* by having Pangloss suggest that God gave us noses to support our spectacles. While this and similar jibes might seem frivolous, they underline a serious objection to this proof *if you insist that what we see in the world today is the crowning achievement of God's design.* Many things that we find useful, such as noses, have achieved the form they have because of natural evolution not because of some *a priori* divine blueprint of the perfect human.

In addition, we have floods, volcanoes, earthquakes, tsunamis, and falling meteors that can wipe out entire species of animals. At first glance, it doesn't seem that these disasters could be a part of a divine plan that makes any sense. Surely the repeated destruction of whole species couldn't possibly be part of a design for some sort of heavenly goal for the universe—unless the operation of evolution, itself, is the mechanism for fulfilling that plan! If you find that idea a little hard to swallow, we'll have more to say about it in the final chapter of this book.

Immanuel Kant (1724-1804): *The Critique of Pure Reason*

It is only when we come to Kant and his monumental work (that incidentally influenced the entire course of philosophy) that we have a more acceptable understanding of what we can and can't prove with our human reason. Of course the 800-plus pages of the *Critique* involve a great deal more than just the ontological, cosmological, and teleological proofs of God's existence, but for the purposes of this discussion we will only consider these proofs here.

The main thrust of Kant's critique of both the ontological and cosmological proofs of God's existence was that one could not draw conclusions about a transcendental being from facts gathered in the physical or non-transcendental world. In the *Critique* he says in his refutation of the ontological argument that all our knowledge of existence is of the present material world, and although another existence beyond this one is possible, *we have no means of ascertaining the truth of its existence.* Therefore, Anselm's so-called proof is no more sufficient than a merchant's wish to increase his wealth by adding zeros to his cash accounts.

So even though we can't rule out the possibility of a transcendent being called God, we have no means to determine His existence by either our *a priori* reason or our *a posteriori* experience of the physical, sensible world. As he says, even though we can use our laws of cause and effect to prove to our own satisfaction that there is an initial cause or a Prime Mover, we have no means of checking to see if our conclusion is correct.

And as for the cosmological proof, the principle that every effect must have a cause is only significant in the sensible world. Even the claim that there can't be an infinite ascending series of causes in the real world is impossible to ascertain and is even more so when attempting to go from the experience in this cosmos, or sphere, to that which is outside it. In a remarkable way this is identical to the statements of modern scientists who say that it is impossible for science to determine what happened before the Big Bang or what caused it. They can determine with a high probability what happened in the nanoseconds *after* it, but they can only guess what happened even a billionth of a nanosecond before it.

But what does Kant say about Aquinas' fifth argument from purpose, the teleological argument? Kant obviously finds this far more convincing than either the ontological or cosmological arguments. In many ways the teleological argument parallels the Anthropic Principle which we discussed in the first chapter. It seems as if we can see in our world "manifest signs of an arrangement full of purpose," and it's hard to imagine that these signs were not designed by a rational entity with a deliberate plan in mind. Therefore, there must exist "a sublime and wise cause (or several), which is not merely a blind, all-powerful nature" which produced it.

However, according to Kant this harmony in the world addresses the form and not the substance of the world. The analogy with human designs cannot apply to the creation of matter as it can to the *design* of matter. So we wind up with an architect of the world but not a creator.

To a 21st Century adult, this doesn't make any sense at all. Why doesn't Kant think that the architect of the world would also be its creator? The reason is that Kant wrote this in the 18th Century and knowledge of the

Big Bang that created the universe wouldn't be known for a couple hundred years. For most thinkers at that time, the universe was infinite and eternal. So detecting purpose in the material world would not mean that you had discovered the one who had created its infinite existence, if indeed you could even imagine that such a being existed. After all, if the universe was infinite and eternal, it had no beginning. No beginning means no creation. But once you have a creation event, then the architect and the creator must be one and the same because the one who started everything going must be the one who designed it.

It should also be pointed out that this was before the 1859 publication of Darwin's *Origin of Species*. Therefore, the "manifest signs of an arrangement full of purpose" that Kant saw about him was the result of millions of years of selective adaptation brought about by the inanimate forces of evolution and not the direct design by a creator of what we see in the world today.

It's tempting to speculate what Kant would have made of the Big Bang and the Anthropic Principle if they had been known before he wrote the *Critique of Pure Reason*. We will never know, but it seems as if there now exists enough evidence to *imply* that the arguments from cause and design may have some merit. Do they prove the existence of God? That, as Kant pointed out, is impossible—just as impossible as it is to prove any of the speculative ideas of some scientists about what happened before the Big Bang. But at the same time, the fact that the universe was created at a specific point in time and that it was finely tuned to guarantee that life could survive and flourish in it gives the proposition that an intelligent entity designed the universe a credibility it hasn't had for four centuries.

A Modern Approach to the Question of God's Existence

As we have pointed out above, in Medieval times the goal was to prove the existence of a God in a cosmology that put the Earth at the center of a static universe. They were trying to prove that God had created all things just as they appeared at that time, a concept supported by Holy Scripture. This put a considerable burden on the ancient clerics and philosophers because they had to talk about creation when there was no creation event to discuss. Everything had existed just as it appeared *ad infinitum*. To be sure all living things went through birth and death life cycles, but nothing else ever changed. Proving God to be the creator of something that was never created in time was an exercise in futility.

Now we have a scientifically-proven creation event of a universe that appears to be meticulously designed to support life. In addition, Darwin's theory of evolution has shown that we posses intelligence because it is a powerful survival trait which must be reflected in the universe, itself. Otherwise, we could never have used it with such great success to understand the universe's natural laws. That implies that *something* that possesses a similar intelligence must have been instrumental in the creation of the universe. To quote Aquinas, "And that *something*, all men call God." Again, does this prove that God exists? Hardly. Science can't be used to prove the existence of anything before the singularity and the Big Bang. However, one thing that it does prove is that believing that God exists and created the universe is a reasonable belief and almost unavoidable for the common-sense view of a rational person.

But does that mean that we have to accept one of the explanations for our existence from one of our current religions? As we will see in the next chapter, that seems highly unlikely in the case of the Judeo/Christian religions when we examine what science and common sense has to say about many of the claims made in the Bible.

Chapter 3
The Bible in Conflict with the Scientific Data

The Conflict About Place

Every major accepted religion in existence today had its beginnings at a time when every civilization thought that the earth was the center of the universe. The ancient Egyptians, Mayans, Mesopotamians, Babylonians, Chinese, Hebrews, Hindus, Romans, Greeks, and all the other early societies could see for themselves that the stars, sun, and moon circled the earth once a day, with just the planets performing their own seemingly random dances across the heavens. No one in his or her right mind would contest the evidence of everyone's eyes.

The founders and major characters of the great religions—Abraham, Moses, Jesus, St. Paul, Buddha, Mohammed, et al.—shared that belief. That's why it was so easy for them and for their followers to believe that this must be some sort of testing ground to determine the fate of each individual. According to the Judeo/Christian traditions, we humans had to atone for the original sin of Adam and Eve either through good works or through the redemption of Jesus on the cross. For the Hindus and Buddhists earth was a training ground where humans had to learn to overcome the wheel of life and death through meditation and right thoughts and actions. A common theme running through all of these theologies is that one's primary purpose in life (and death) is to escape this veil of pain and tears one way or another. Either we opted for God's kingdom on earth where all the good folks lived happily ever after and all the bad ones went to Hell, or we looked forward to a celestial kingdom in Heaven, or to absorption into Brahma, or to achieving Nirvana.

When Copernicus and Galileo made their devastating claim that the center of the universe was the sun and not the earth, the testing-ground theory was put in jeopardy. Once you lump earth with all the other planets, it's no longer a stable platform at center stage but a moving planet, no different from any other planet. Earth loses its primary position in the universe and is replaced by the entire solar system.

Now we know that the sun is not only *not* the center of the universe, it isn't even a very significant star among billions of stars in our galaxy, the Milky Way. And in the last century we have discovered that our galaxy is only one of billions of galaxies, each containing billions of more stars, most of which presumably contain planetary systems similar to our own. As Carl Sagan put it:

> ...we live on an insignificant planet of a humdrum star
> lost between two spiral arms in the outskirts of a galaxy
> which is a member of a sparse cluster of galaxies, tucked
> away in some forgotten corner of a universe in which
> there are far more galaxies than people.[1]

That's one huge mouthful, but it does say it all. Our entire solar system is
no more significant than one of the grains of sand in the Sahara desert, as
the Hubble image below shows (all images are galaxies except the star near
the center). Did God really create all this because He was lonely and
wanted a man to talk to as it says in the Bible?

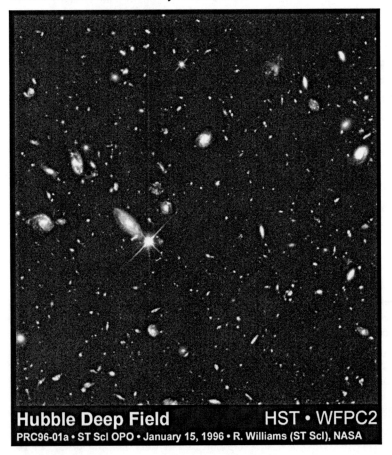

Hubble Deep Field   **HST • WFPC2**
PRC96-01a • ST ScI OPO • January 15, 1996 • R. Williams (ST ScI), NASA

The Conflict About Time

Unfortunately for the biblical literalists, it doesn't end there since
we have also discovered that this universe of ours isn't just a few thousand

---

[1] Sagan, Carl; *Cosmos*, Random House, New York, 1980; p. 193.

years old as implied in the Bible but about 13.7 billion years old. Furthermore, life on planet Earth started about four billion years ago and gradually evolved into the dinosaurs, which became the dominant life forms on the earth for about 140 million years without a human in sight! At least that's what the fossil record seems to say, and there are literally tons of bones to support that thesis. It wasn't until about 65 million years ago when a meteor presumably slammed into the earth that these highly successful creatures were wiped out allowing our mammalian ancestors to evolve. The earliest human remains and stone tools are no more than a couple of million years old, the earliest evidence of farming a hundred thousand years old, and the earliest evidence of a written language only a few thousand years old.

If we equate the approximate age of the universe to be equivalent to the length of a football field from one goal line to the other, the amount of time that we humans and our direct ancestors, *Homo sapiens*, existed would be represented by little more than the width of a toothpick on the final goal line. We don't even look so important when compared to how long the dinosaurs have been around. The half a million years of *Homo sapiens'* life span is less than one-half of one percent of the length of time the dinosaurs roamed the earth.

Obviously, things did not start with us. In fact, things have been going along for an immense period of time before we were even a twinkle in God's eye. If you want to reconcile religion and the data, you will have to admit that God created our earth billions of years before He created us. Why?

The Conflict About Geology

The separation between the biblical account and the archeological record widens even further. The several ice ages for which there is a great deal of evidence are not mentioned in the Bible, but the Bible does recount the story of a simultaneous world-wide flood for which there is no evidence. However there is evidence of great regional flooding when the glaciers melted after the last ice age and ice barriers suddenly collapsed sending tons of water flooding the plains and raising the level of land-locked seas so that their coastal areas were inundated. But the rest of the landscape was left pretty much the way we see it today.

Now let's consider the Great Flood as recounted in the Bible. It says Noah put his family and all the animals "two by two" in an ark that he and his sons built before it rained over the entire earth for 40 days and 40 nights. Then the Bible says that the waters "receded" until dry land reappeared and Noah and his entourage could disembark and reestablish life on Earth.

If there was a flood that covered the entire globe, where did it recede to?

In fact, where did all that water come from in the first place? If you say that it evaporated from the oceans, a truly stupendous amount of water would have had to evaporate simultaneously from all the oceans and form as clouds. If such an evaporation took place—an action for which there is no evidence and no theory as to why it would—the oceans would drop accordingly. Then the amount of water coming down during the 40 days would simply put back the water that had been taken from the oceans in the first place. All the highlands would remain highlands, uncovered by water. Things would get soggy, and there would be many local and regional floods before the water had a chance to run off and reenter the oceans. But it would certainly not wipe out all life on earth except for Noah and the people and animals on his relatively tiny boat.

Then there's the problem of the animals Noah supposedly saved . What happened to the kangaroos and koala bears (Australia), pandas (China), Emperor Penguins (Antarctica), polar bears (Alaska), snow leopards (Himalayas), and North American buffaloes? I can guarantee that none of them nor thousands of other species were on Noah's little boat thousands of miles away in the middle East. How did they survive?

But let's just go along with the story and accept that this is God's miracle and He could presumably make the rain come down miraculously from God-made clouds. The most rain in a 24-hour period that has ever been recorded was 74 inches at Cilaos (on the Indian Ocean island of Reunion) between 15 and 16 March 1952. That's a little over 3 inches per hour. In Jacksonville, FL, however, 5 inches were recorded in one hour on May 27, 1975. But this is God's rain so we can suppose that He could make it rain 12 inches per hour for as long as it took to cover all the mountains around the world. That would be like living night and day under a waterfall for however long it took to finish the job.

The highest mountain in the world is Mt. Everest at about 29,000 ft. Therefore, at a foot per hour it would take the rain 29,000 hours to cover it, or over 3-1/4 years. But even if we just consider Mt. Ararat[2] at about 19,000 ft. above sea level, it would still take 19,000 hours to cover the peak, or over 2 years. How could Noah, his family, and all the animals survive on the food they could possibly carry on their little boat? And with a continuous cloud covering the entire globe for all that time, it would be very much like the predicted nuclear winter that would result from an atomic war. Noah and his boat would undoubtedly be buried under a glacier of ice after the rain—or more accurately, the snow and sleet—stopped.

The biblical story is very easy to accept when it's set in a cosmos where the Earth is a flat, rectangular land floating on the "firmament" with all the heavenly bodies circling around it. And since the people living at the time this story originated knew nothing of the mechanism of evaporation that causes rain, they could easily accept a continuous rain coming from the

---

[2] Where presumably Noah landed his boat after the flood.

same mysterious rain clouds where all the other rain came from. And of course it would run off the edges of the world into the firmament when the rain stopped. The animals would be those that were available within the bounds of their known world, a limited group that could easily fit into a boat that could be built by Noah and his sons. But when the story is set on a global world many hundreds of thousands times larger than their little rectangular known piece of land, it becomes a fairy tale and just a story about a big local flood. There would still be plenty of people and animals left in the world when it ended.

Some of you may think that I'm beating a dead horse here, but the truth is that there are a startling number of people who believe quite literally in the Great Flood story despite these obvious problems with it. Even one of our astronauts went searching for Noah's Ark after he left the space program. It shows the extremes which even intelligent people are willing to go to in order to cling to the belief that the Bible contains an accurate account of events in our past.

The Conflict About Moses and His Miracles

It would have been very interesting to be present when Pharaoh's daughter came into the palace with her story about finding a little baby floating down the stream. I'm sure all the members of Pharaoh's court judiciously went along with his beloved daughter's story, but in the privacy of their villas I would be surprised if knowing winks weren't exchanged.

Now consider this scenario: Here's a boy who is probably—at least in the minds of those in the Pharaoh's court—the illegitimate grandson of the undisputed leader of the greatest superpower of the land. Judging from all the things that Moses accomplished during his lifetime, he undoubtedly had an IQ that would knock your socks off. While he was growing up, he had free run of a palace that contained a group of priests known for their feats of legerdemain. This "ward" of the ruling family commanded the tolerance of all who encountered him, but few of the priests would fear his presence in their midst since he would never have a position of power in the hierarchy. It is interesting to speculate what a bright inquisitive boy like this would pick up from what he overheard in the halls of the priestly elect.

Shamans and priests the world over have learned how to explain periodic disasters like floods, draughts, and earthquakes as actions of the gods angered at the behavior of their subjects. If the people would only do what the priests tell them to do, these things wouldn't happen to them. And in the case of the Egyptian priests they were also skilled at slight-of-hand tricks that could turn walking sticks into snakes.

Now when Moses, who knew that at least his father was a Jew, saw an Egyptian beating a Hebrew, he killed the Egyptian and ran into the desert to escape punishment. It was there that he said he saw a burning bush and had a conversation with God, who called himself I AM WHO SAYS I AM, and received special powers to turn rods into snakes. Of course, no one but Moses witnessed all this, so we have to take his word for it, but an awful lot of people believe it happened just as he said. However, if you have a skeptic's frame of mind, you might say to yourself, "Now isn't that amazing that God gave Moses the same kind of magical powers that the Egyptian priests had!" And when Moses went back into Egypt to free the Jews after the Pharaoh died, he had a magical duel with the Egyptian priests, using those very same powers. But even though he won the duel when his snake ate their snakes, the new Pharaoh still wouldn't let his people go.

That was something that always puzzled me as a kid. Why wouldn't Pharaoh be terrified of the power of this man's God? Moses claimed it was his God who imposed plagues and pestilences on the land when Pharaoh wouldn't let his people go. But of course, since Pharaoh had seen his priests turn rods into snakes and saw them crediting their own gods for catastrophes, why should he be scared when Moses used the same excuse?

A recent PBS documentary claimed that all of this happened around 1500 B.C.E. when the Santorini volcano erupted in a gigantic explosion. The gases that were escaping during its pre-eruption earthquake period could have accounted for all ten plagues, even the death of the first-borne male Egyptians when low-lying carbon-dioxide gas smothered these boys as they slept in their privileged position on the ground floor of their homes. Fascinating if true.

In any case, Moses and the Hebrews were eventually able to leave Egypt when Pharaoh finally gave in, probably when the volcano finally blew its top. But after they left, Pharaoh changed his mind and sent his troops after them to bring them back.

That's when Moses parted the Red Sea in his most spectacular miracle.

It should be pointed out that disastrous tsunamis can result from earthquakes, mudslides, and—most interestingly for us—volcanoes. I doubt that Moses foresaw that a tsunami would result from the eruption, but when the water receded from the shore, he seized on the opportunity and led his people over the water-softened sand that could trap the narrow wheels of Pharaoh's chariots. I imagine everybody was already running like crazy and they certainly wouldn't have stopped until they got to the opposite shore. When Moses saw the waters rushing back, all he had to do was take advantage of the situation, raise his staff, and call the waters to return and wipe out their pursuers. That's something no one would ever forget.

After that the Bible says that they were guided by a pillar of fire by night and a pillar of clouds by day—in other words, they used another volcano to the East as their reference point for the direction they should take to flee from Egypt. Lots of things happened to them on their long trek through the desert, but the one of greatest significance was the creation of the Ten Commandments.

When they came to the mountain called Mt. Sinai, it apparently was still active in a post-eruption mode since the Bible says that God descended on the mountain with fire and hid his face with clouds of smoke. When Moses got tired of solving all the disputes of the people, he said that God told him to go up the mountain to get some rules from Him that they all could follow. So up he went and stayed for the regulation 40 days and 40 nights—certainly a strangely long time for God to compose His commandments. (A skeptic might suggest that Moses needed the time to chisel the commandments out of the stone.) To make a long story short, he comes down from the mountain, finds the Hebrews worshiping a golden calf, smashes the tablets, and slays all the backsliders. Then he has to go back up the mountain and do it all over again. We obviously don't know what was on the original set, but when the new tablets came down, the first three out of the ten commandments emphasized that they couldn't go around worshiping graven images like golden calves and that they must pay allegiance to the One God that got them out of their terrible bondage in the first place.

Of course, all of this is mere speculation, but to my mind it explains the miracles of Moses in a much more reasonable way than the account given in the Bible. And if Moses did all this as a human being, he emerges as an incredibly exceptional leader and a genius of the first rank rather than as a puppet of a God that was pulling all the strings.

The Conflict About Human Origins

And then there's the really tough question. Were the original man and woman created with God's own hands out of mud and one of Adam's ribs, possessed with full-blown intelligence, a fully developed language with which they communicated with God and each other, and complete familiarity with tool making, the principles of farming, and a knowledge of animal husbandry? The Bible either states explicitly that this is the case, or it implies it because the stories which follow the account of the Fall talk of Adam and Eve's sons working in the fields and having domesticated animals.

But the fossil record doesn't agree with this scheme of things, and that's true no matter what theory of creation or evolution you accept.

The period that deals most directly with this problem is the Stone Age that extends from about two million years ago to 10,000 or 5,000 years ago depending on the region. It is currently divided into three general eras: the Paleolithic or Old Stone Age which was the longest and lasted until the end of the last ice age in about 13,000 B.C.E. ; the Mesolithic or Middle Stone Age occurred during the more clement weather and lasted until about 8,000 B.C.E.; and the Neolithic or New Stone Age extended until about

5,000 B.C.E. During the Paleolithic period, mentally aware creatures with human-like skeletons created stone tools by pounding on them with other stones until they assumed useful shapes, such as axes and spear heads. The later periods are characterized by flaked tools which were much more difficult to produce but also much more useful cutting implements. By hitting a piece of flint at just the right angle, a "flake" of stone will split from the original, allowing the stone to be carefully shaped. The resulting products have extremely sharp edges and are far superior cutting tools than the old crudely pounded-out stones. Since they can be made thin and light, they can be attached to smaller wooden shafts to make throwing spears or arrows, formidable weapons and considerably safer than the Paleolithic hand-held stabbing spear which required the spear carrier to be within the range of the claws and teeth of large, enraged animals.

The evidence from the sites where these beings lived indicates that they survived primarily by killing and eating animals and by gathering fruit and berries. There is no evidence of the grain that would result from farming or any tools that could be used for tilling the soil or harvesting the wheat. It isn't until between 9000 and 5000 B.C.E. in Southeast Asia that there is any evidence of the cultivation of wheat and barley along with the domestication of animals. This means we are faced with over two million years of evidence of human-like activity and human-like skeletons, with the gradual improvement of tool-making techniques, until we finally get to the point where humans can be found who actually "tilled the soil," as the Bible says, or tended domesticated animals. Up until that time, humans had been hunter-gatherers, not farmers.

Evidence of language is harder to come by for the simple reason that humans undoubtedly communicated verbally long before they invented writing or at least put it in a form that would survive the ages. The earliest writings we have found occurred many centuries after the first evidence of farming.

So here we have the dilemma. If God created man and woman complete with language and knowledge of farming and animal husbandry, when did He drop these fully completed humans on earth? Or if they were already on earth in some as yet undiscovered Eden, when were they banned and started to leave evidence of their existence? It can't be in the early Paleolithic or Neolithic Periods because there is no evidence of farming during those periods. If they appeared during the later period where there is evidence of farming and animal husbandry, who were the beings that occupied the earth during the previous stone ages and displayed such an abundant evidence of human-like activities and human-like remains?

It should be noted that in all of this discussion, not once did we mention Darwin or any theory of evolution. It isn't the theories that are the problem, it's the physical evidence. It is literally impossible to accept the biblical account of Adam and Eve as the prototype humans if we are going to accept any of this overwhelming evidence to the contrary. Either you're going to have to accept the biblical creation stories as religious myth, unrelated to the way life evolved on this earth, or you're going to have to claim that the tons of evidence to the contrary don't exist and that the scientific method is invalid. Your choice.

But now it's time to take a closer look at what the Darwin theory of evolution is and how it developed. For the naturalists of the 18th and 19th Centuries it was a very welcome and reasonable explanation for why there was so much evidence that species were evolving gradually and naturally.

Darwin's Simple Solution

Over one-hundred years before Darwin published his famous *Origin of Species* in 1859 some naturalists realized that the gradual changes they observed in species could not be explained by the prevailing creation stories of biblical origin. The Bible claimed that all life forms were created separately and immutably; that is, they were unable to change from their original form. The 18th and early 19th century naturalists realized that species not only gradually mutated within themselves, but that this mutation implied that they might very well produce different species through transmutations. Georges-Louis Leclerc, Comte de Buffon (1707-1788) in his *Historie Naturelle* was the first to openly suggest that the similarities between Man and apes may indicate a common ancestry and that the planet was much older than the 6,000 years claimed by the Church. Unfortunately, he didn't suggest a mechanism for explaining such an evolution. Most rejected his ideas because of the prevailing Church-supported view that all creatures had been created independently of one another by God.

When in 1793 Jean-Baptiste Lamarck (1744-1829) started studying insects and worms—that is, the "invertebrates," a term he coined himself—it was perhaps inevitable that their much shorter life spans than that of the vertebrates would allow him to note the variety of mutations within their species because their mutations from one generation to the next occurred so much faster. Up until this time few naturalists had considered the invertebrates worthy of study. Lamarck postulated in his 1809 thesis, *Philosophie Zoologique*, that natural law may have been the cause of these mutations. As Darwin noted in the Preface to the *Origin*:

> [Lamarck] first did the eminent service of arousing attention to the probability of all change in the organic, as well as in the inorganic world, being the result of law, and not of miraculous interposition. Lamarck seems to have been chiefly led to his conclusion on the gradual change of species, by the difficulty of distinguishing species and varieties, by the almost perfect gradation of forms in

certain groups, and by the analogy of domestic productions.[3]

Lamarck suggested that the natural agent for producing these mutations was habit, so that consistent habits of one generation were passed on to the next, enhancing the appropriate physical characteristics in the process—a theory known as the "inheritance of acquired traits."[4] Lamarck never received recognition for his work in his lifetime and is largely ignored today because no one can come up with a reason why habit would result in mutation. But he was at least the first to look for a natural explanation for the gradual mutation of species. Once the age of the world was determined to be in the millions or even billions of years—allowing nature the time needed to make significant changes by gradual mutation—the stage was set for the brilliant yet simple solution for the natural creation of species put forward by Darwin and Wallace half a century later.

By the time Darwin was preparing his definitive book, numerous papers had been presented in naturalist circles on evolution, the hot new topic inspired by increasing evidence of mutation within species. Up to this time, however, no one could point to a mechanism that would account for the natural changes. As we have said, the accepted dogma was that God created species that were perfect for their function in their allotted environment and were thus immutable. Naturalists questioned that thesis at their peril, not only risking the termination of their professional careers but the scorn and condemnation of their Christian brethren. Yet the steamroller of evidence would not be denied.

In 1858, Alfred Russell Wallace circulated a paper entitled, "On the Tendency of Varieties to Depart Indefinitely from the Original Type." It put Darwin in something of a panic because it was obvious that Wallace had discovered the mechanism for natural selection in parallel with Darwin. On the advice of friends and colleagues, Darwin put an end to his interminable procrastination and published the *Origin of Species*. If he had hesitated again, fundamentalists today would be condemning Wallace's theory of evolution and not Darwin's. Again, it wasn't the man and a particular theory that was the problem. Mutation within species was leading to the obvious conclusion that species, themselves, could be the result of transmutations. Once a reasonable natural explanation for this was proposed, the idea that each individual species was divinely created just as we see them today was impossible to maintain.

---

[3] See http://www.literature.org/authors/darwin-charles/the-origin-of-species/preface.html. By "domestic productions" Darwin means the human practice of breeding for certain characteristics among horses, dogs, and cattle.

[4] Thus, for example, the giraffes' *habit* of reaching for the higher more succulent leaves would supposedly make their offspring's necks longer in subsequent generations. No one has ever found a scientific explanation for why habits could be the cause of changes in the physical forms of animals and passed from one generation to the next.

Darwin's and Wallace's simple idea was that natural selection allowed certain reproductive mutations to flourish in changing environmental conditions while the original form had difficulty adapting and eventually died out. In particular, it had been noted that sometimes individuals within species exhibited variations in the characteristics of the regular members. When the environment changed, if one type of chance variation had a survival and reproductive advantage in the new environment, these better-adapted characteristics tended to increase in frequency in the population. This meant that they had a better chance of sexual union with the ones who had the more successful genes, thereby passing those genes on to future generations.

Darwin observed this process in his epochal trip aboard the ship *The Beagle* in the 1830's when he examined the similarities and *differences* among the tortoises, finches, and other flora and fauna on each of the Galapagos Islands off South America. It seemed obvious that they had adapted to the different conditions found on each island. [5]

This was the reason Darwin's theory was so rapidly accepted among the naturalists. It gave a simple and obvious reason for mutations to occur. One noted naturalist berated himself for not thinking of such an obvious solution to the problem of natural selection when it was almost staring him in the face. After all, humans had been doing their own selective breeding for generations, which resulted in such widely divergent breeds as Chihuahuas and Great Danes from wild wolves.

Contrary to what fundamentalists believe, naturalists accepted Darwin's ideas so quickly, not because of their admiration for Darwin or their appreciation of a theory that allowed them to explain the variety of species without referring to Holy Scripture, but because it explained the evidence that had become so apparent over the previous century. As we said, by accepting evolution, these professionals were putting their careers on the line as well as their social standing in their communities. This was an idea that was in direct opposition to the cherished beliefs of the vast majority of all citizens in the western world, not just Christians. They risked becoming pariahs because Darwin's theory so beautifully explained the facts in an obvious and logical way.

That's why comparing Darwin's evolution with creationism is comparing apples to oranges. Darwin's theory isn't designed to prove that species mutate. Mutation of species is a fact, not a theory. The theory only explains *why* they mutate. Creationism doesn't address that problem because it mistakenly claims that there is no mutation to explain. It says that all things, vegetable and animal, were created directly by God just as we see them today. So the creationists need to explain why scientists have

---

[5] See http://www.pbs.org/wgbh/evolution/darwin/origin/index.html for an excellent example of bird mutations in different environments. This entire web site is an excellent presentation of the theory of evolution and its development over the years.

discovered mutations when the biblical doctrine or "theory" claims that there are none to discover. But if we evolved through natural selection, where does that leave the Bible?

The Biblical Creation Stories as Myth

If we accept the creation stories as myth and not as fact, then we won't have to worry about the discrepancies with the physical evidence. Gone is the ridiculous requirement that we believe this universe with its billions upon billions of stars existing for billions upon billions of years was created so that a man and woman on a tiny planet in an insignificant galaxy could be tempted to eat an apple! Nor do we have to accept the other[6] biblical creation story as literal fact where God created the earth in seven days with still no mention of the trillions of stars or the mind-boggling billions of years that the universe existed before man came along.

There are many perceptive Christians and Jews who are fully aware that the Bible can't be used as a realistic source of information about the universe, but who still think their religion's theology is valid. The trouble is that one can't shrug off the biblical discrepancies so easily without questioning the entire premise of the Judeo/Christian religions; i.e., that humanity is a "fallen" species which is sinful by nature. This is the whole point of the Adam and Eve creation story and for their banishment from the Garden of Eden for eating the forbidden fruit. In the Christian religions it is also the basis for the redemption theory of humankind by the crucifixion of Jesus Christ. According to the latter, the only reason God allowed His only Son to be crucified was to redeem the world from original sin. Many may think that makes sense[7] when it's possible to believe the Adam and Eve story literally, but as soon as that's reclassified as a myth, original sin has to become undefined and meaningless even to believers. Was *Homo habilis* ("handy man") sinful for descending from the trees and inventing tools? Was *Homo erectus* ("upright man") sinful because he stood upright? And finally, was our direct ancestor, *Homo sapiens* ("wise man"), sinful because he could reason? Which version of mankind "fell" from grace?

You can see why the fundamentalists fear evolution so much, whether it's explained by Darwin's theory or someone else's. Gradual development of humanity is anathema to anyone believing that we are a fully developed species that fell from some righteous (or at least better)

---

[6] Biblical scholars agree that there are two creation stories in Genesis. The first in Genesis 1:1 to 2:4a was written during or after the Jews' Babylonian captivity. The second in Genesis 2:4b to 2:25 was written many centuries before.

[7] Although I must confess that I have always been puzzled by the idea that a God could correct His ill-tempered act of extreme punishment for a minor offense by having His only Son tortured and killed by the same beings that committed the original offense! Who's being redeemed in such a crazy scenario, humanity or God?

position in the cosmological scheme of things. Not only does gradualism contradict the creation story of the Bible, it also questions the entire theology of Christianity—Protestant, Catholic, and Eastern Orthodox. That means we must accept the possibility that two thousand years of religious ecstasy, mysticism, hope, beauty, awesome architecture, exquisite art, and inspired music along with wars, genocides, inquisitions, stake-burnings, fear, and misery were accomplished or committed for all the wrong reasons. It's not the first time that's happened in human history and it won't be the last.

Is the Adam and Eve Myth just a Fabrication?

Until fairly recently, the word "myth" has had a very bad press. Most people assumed it meant "charming lie" and treated it accordingly. That is, they did until people like Carl Jung and Joseph Campbell, et al., proposed that some myths were actually stories which reflected a kind of truth that existed in the human psyche. Those truths in many cases seemed to be universal and consistent throughout various cultures even though the specific details of the stories varied depending on the society in which they were told.

In addition, there were some stories which could have been a mythical or storyteller's interpretation of an event which actually happened. A good example is the tale of the capture and eventual rescue of Helen of Troy. For years historians considered Homer's *Iliad* to be a work of fiction. It wasn't until the German amateur archeologist Heinrich Schliemann excavated the ruins of Troy in 1870 that scholars began to take at least the part of the tale that told of the Trojan War as possibly historically accurate. Up to that time, even the existence of the ancient city of Troy was considered to be a fabrication.

Could the Adam and Eve story be derived from a real event? Surprisingly enough, some recent discoveries in anthropology and genetics may (and I emphasize *may*) shed some light on it.

If we consider genetics, it seems that there is more than one kind of DNA in the human cell that can tell us something about our ancestors. Besides the recombinant DNA found in the nucleus of a cell, there is another DNA only found in women in what is called the *mitochondria organelle* (where an organelle might be thought of as a tiny organ that performs dedicated functions within cells).

This mitochondrial DNA (mtDNA) can only change by gradual mutation over decades and is inherited only from the mother, not the father. MtDNA does not participate in sexual reproduction like the nuclear DNA and does not undergo recombination with the male sperm's DNA. Because there is no sexual recombination where the history of the gene is partially lost in each recombination between male and female genes, the mtDNA only evolves gradually and can be used to study genetic lineages within families—even the vast and ancient human family. Indeed, it has been established that *all humans bear mitochondrial DNA from a single ancestral female.*

Enter the Mitochondrial Eve

In 1987 the media announced that we all descended from a "mitochondrial Eve." That statement is incredibly misleading because it implies that we descended from the biblical Eve who was the only female in existence on earth at the time. Nothing could be further from the truth. If a mother has no children or bears only sons, her mtDNA becomes extinct. Therefore, her mtDNA would never be passed along to future generations.

For example, if five couples were marooned on an island and one gave birth to four females who were mated to males from the other couples, their progeny would have only one mtDNA ancestral matron no matter how many generations came after her. As far as the other couples are concerned, if each woman only has male heirs, their mtDNA is lost. If the original matron has only one daughter, the daughter, rather than the mother, becomes the original ancestral matron or "Eve" as far as we can determine from genetic data. If the other couples have females who are matriarchs of family lines which eventually die out or produce only males, their mtDNA disappears as well. So this technique does not, and cannot, indicate how many females were present in her day, and it certainly doesn't imply that she was the only one and therefore the first one, the biblical Eve. However, in genetic terms it does mean that she and her descendants were certainly the most successful at staying alive and producing enough females to pass along their matriarch's mtDNA to the present day!

Which brings us back to our original question in this section: Does the Adam and Eve story reflect some ancient reality? With the aid of the mitochondrial DNA and the fossil record we can certainly make some interesting speculations.

The original study examined the mtDNA in a number of women of different nationality and origin and came to the conclusion that since mtDNA slowly accumulates mutations over time and Africans had the largest number of mutations, the mtDNA Eve must have come from Africa. Furthermore, by making estimates about the number of mutations which could occur from one generation to the next, they calculated that she must have existed between 140,000 and 290,000 years ago, about the same time as the first known appearance of anatomically modern humans in the fossil record!

However, although some additional studies have supported the original dates and origins, others using different mutation rates have produced dates for the mtDNA Eve ranging all the way from less than 100,000 years ago to 500,000 years. In addition, the out-of-Africa hypothesis has been debated strenuously by some scientists who prefer a multiple origin for *Homo sapiens* rather than a single one. In light of the Darwinian thesis of evolution which holds that new species evolved through very successful "mistakes" in the gene pool, this multi-regional hypothesis is hard to justify when it requires an identical mistake or series of mistakes to occur among many different tribes in widely separated, dissimilar environments.

Evidence from the Fossil Record

We can also look at the fossil record for evidence of place of origin. Within the last 30 years a significant number of fossils of early human-like remains have been discovered. The ones believed to be the first human ancestors—the first creatures of the genus *Homo* ("Man")—created tools, lived from about 2.2 to 1.6 million years ago, and have been given the name *Homo habilis*, or handy man. There is great diversity among the fossil remains of these earliest humans, leading anthropologists to take the view that although modern humans evolved from one single branch of the evolutionary tree, there were many branches that existed in the formative years of mankind's development which died out.

In 1891 a longer-legged species of *Homo habilis* was found in Java and subsequently named *Homo erectus* for its posture and ability to walk upright. These individuals had considerably larger skulls, and thus larger brains, than *Homo habilis*, and the shape of their skulls indicates that they might have been able to talk. In 1976 a complete *Homo erectus* skull 1.5 million years old was discovered in East Africa, indicating that this was the original evolutionary birthplace of *Homo erectus*, which subsequently spread out over Europe and Asia during the next million years.

Homo sapiens, the "wise men" whose brain capacity, skull shape, and skeletal shape were approximately the same as ours apparently came on the scene about 300,000 years ago and spread rapidly throughout Europe and Asia. Not only did they spread rapidly but they apparently became the dominant species in a relatively short span of time. Taking the admittedly shaky dating for the mtDNA Eve and the current dating for the emergence of *Homo sapiens* in the fossil record, the rough concurrence of the two can be suggestive.

However, there is still controversy surrounding the identity of the particular branch of *Homo sapiens* that led to us. For example, there is the question of the lineage of the *Homo sapiens* found in the Neander Valley in Germany, the *Neanderthals*, who appear on the scene about 300,000 years ago and died out about 30,000 B.C.E. One school of thought believes that we are descended from them, while another believes that they were one of the unsuccessful branches. Since there is evidence supporting both theses, the jury is still out on this question, forcing us to wait for additional evidence to resolve it definitively one way or the other.[8]

This type of controversy has caused some anthropologists to classify modern humans as a subspecies of *Homo sapiens* called *Homo sapiens sapiens*. For our purposes this is ideal because we don't have to worry about whether or not we are in a direct lineage to Neanderthal or any other type of *Homo sapiens*, but can simply take note that while they are very similar to us, they also exhibit a few distinctly different physical and behavioral characteristics.

For example, physically the arm and leg bones of Neanderthal were twice as thick as ours and although their prominent noses, long faces, and big skulls were similar to ours, the size of their skulls was larger and their configuration was quite different with a smaller forebrain and poorly developed speech areas. Their bodies were ideally adapted for a species living during an ice age because their short, stocky form conserved heat. Our forms are better suited for the warmer climates closer to the Equator.

The real difference, though, lies in their behavior patterns. Although hundreds of Neanderthal individuals have been found along with their artifacts, their simple but effective tools varied little over the 270,000 years or so of their existence. Compare that to our own history. At first the artifacts or tool kits of *Homo sapiens sapiens* varied little from Neanderthal's. But soon after that, they showed a tendency to change very rapidly over time. To get a feel for the vast difference between the two species, consider the amount of changes that have occurred in the tools and artifacts of the human race from 10,000 B.C.E. through the Copper, Bronze, and Iron Ages to the beginning of the Common Era. Even though the Neanderthals had 27 times 10,000 years to make the simplest of changes to their tools, they made very few significant changes at all![9]

...And now Back to the Story of Adam and Eve

At this point we leave the relative certainty of science and enter the realm of pure speculation. But that's where the Adam and Eve story becomes very interesting, indeed.

The basic elements of the Adam and Eve story are these: (1) Adam and Eve were originally in an idyllic garden where they wanted for nothing—all was supplied by a benevolent God or ruler/creator of the garden. (2)There was a source of knowledge, symbolized by an apple tree, the fruit of which was taboo for anyone to consume. (3) Eve claimed that an

---

[8] Recent DNA studies have shown that there is considerable difference between some short strings of Neanderthal's DNA and ours. But since these Neanderthal DNA strings are so short, there is still no definitive proof that we are not related.

[9] You might call this a stunning misapplication of the old adage, "if it ain't broke, don't fix it!"

external agent, symbolized by a snake,[10] convinced her to persuade Adam to join her in consuming the forbidden fruit (i.e., knowledge). (4) Once they consumed the apple(s), they realized they were naked so they hid from God. When (5) God, the ruler/creator of the garden, realized they had consumed the forbidden fruit, he banished them forever from the idyllic garden and condemned them to a short life of misery and pain.

Now lets map that mythical story on to what could have been the situation 130,000 to 150,000 years ago. A tribe of *Homo sapiens* who had not significantly changed their habits or tools for tens of thousands of years was holed up in a nice warm cave or protected valley. In this small group of individuals, innovation in anything was not looked upon with favor— you could say that the "knowledge tree" of innovation was forbidden. Into this group was born an individual, at least one of the first *Homo sapiens sapiens*, who was different from the others. Eventually, as this person produced children, his or her descendants also exhibited even more of these differences and were gradually shunned by the "normal" members of the tribe. If during this particular time it was discovered that this strange group had developed different weapons, clothes, artifacts, or techniques while the rest of the tribe relied on the "old" ways, the conflict between the two groups would probably have escalated until their chief/king/shaman banned them from their comfortable, safe home—their Eden.

We can assume that our mtDNA Eve was a member of this group. Whether she was the original Eve of the story or not, as we said before, we can't tell from the genetic record, but she was definitely a very early member of the group. And in addition, although I have posited a group of *Homo sapiens sapiens* being thrown out, it could just as easily been only the first such family, keeping our imaginative scenario more closely aligned with the original story. However, their chances of survival would have been significantly reduced, and we would still be left with the problem of where the wives of Adam and Eve's sons and grandsons came from (as described in the third chapter of Genesis).

Thus throughout the ages from the time of the original expulsion from that comfortable, safe cave or valley, we have been plagued by the story of the original sin of our ancestors and their responsibility for our short miserable lives. It's certainly easy to look back on the old days as better than the way things are in the present, and it's even easier the farther back we go. But I venture to guess that even a few generations after the expulsion, not many *Homo sapiens sapiens* would have found the old life with the original *Homo sapiens* very attractive, even though their new life

---

[10] An interesting variation to this story can be found in the text called the Testimony of Truth uncovered in 1945 at Nag Hammadi that tells it from the point of view of the serpent (!), who in Gnostic literature is the principle of divine wisdom. In this version Eve has been convinced by the symbol of universal knowledge to persuade Adam to use his brain, while the Lord is jealously trying to prevent it to protect his status!

away from the old sanctuary was difficult and fraught with danger. The rapidity with which the new species replaced or assimilated the old is proof that the "good old days" weren't nearly good enough, no matter how much we yearned for them or how guilty we felt about leaving them.

But that guilt has stayed with us for all these thousands of years and severely colored the way we have looked at ourselves and our environment. According to the Judeo/Christian view of things, we live in this physical world of hardship and pain because of our "original sin" and can only escape it when we die and either ascend to Heaven, descend to Hell, or are one of the chosen to be raised from the dead at the coming of the Kingdom of God. That makes us rather wretched creatures whose only hope is to be forgiven by an all-powerful God in order to escape this nasty place and get back to our lovely Eden. A pretty pathetic scenario if all we did was to become smarter than a tribe of creatures with limited intelligence and less imagination.

So Where does that Leave Us?

This imaginary scenario about the "true" Adam and Eve story is indeed mere speculation, but the fossil record implies that something like it may very well have happened when *Homo sapiens sapiens* came on the scene. The timing of the appearance of the original mitochondrial Eve and her place of origin may still be debated in the scientific community, but few would claim that she didn't exist. And the complete and almost instantaneous (as far as geological time is concerned) domination of our species in the world of the humanoids is without question. We are the only species of the genus *Homo* remaining in the world (with apologies to Big Foot and the Himalayan Yeti for not believing in their existence).

What is in question is how we got here and how we assumed our role as the dominant species. Did God give it to us at the time of our creation out of the mud as it says in Genesis? There is overwhelming evidence that He didn't. Our species didn't suddenly appear, fully developed with an articulate language, knowledge of animal husbandry and farming, and a tool-making capability of unprecedented complexity. There is too much physical evidence that has to be swept under the rug if we are to cling with desperation to the biblical account of our creation.

But what about Darwin's theory of evolution? Does it really imply that there is no purpose in the universe and that everything has been predetermined by mechanical, natural laws? It is characteristic of humans to rush to accept a theory as an explanation for everything when it is as alluring as Darwin's theory—especially when it seems to support a prior conviction that everything is predetermined. Here is seeming proof positive that everything in this world is governed by mechanical, natural laws. The determinists were right up to a point. But...

...Sometimes the Pendulum Swings Too Far!

A case in point is *The Selfish Gene* written by Charles Dawkins, a hugely successful book that's guilty of the same conceit of many of the more literal-minded Christians and Jews: Dawkins anthropomorphizes the gene just as some religionists anthropomorphize God—in other words, he assigns human design to inanimate molecules.

The odd thing is that he can do this and actually get away with it because it explains evolution very nicely. You can say that genes do indeed seem to "act" as if they are deliberately trying to assure their own survival, using the human form as a throwaway survival mechanism necessary only for the gene's group survival. To be sure, Dawkins takes great pains to assure the reader that he is fully aware that a gene has no more emotion than a lump of clay. But then he proceeds throughout the rest of his book as if genes are just as motivated and capable of changing external events as you or I.

Although this approach makes evolution fun to read and think about, it ignores what this seeming intelligence implies about the very mechanism for evolution. Consider Darwin's main thesis: life forms are altered over time because environmental pressures make the selection of certain chance variations in their genes more probable when they are better suited for survival under the new conditions. So it is the external conditions and "mistakes" in the DNA molecule that lead to successful continuation of the species, not the deliberate machinations of the genes. But if in reality genes *seem* to be intelligent, what does that imply about the changing environment and the "chance" alterations of DNA? Could it be that there is some intelligence and purpose behind the very nature of our universe?

All life forms strive to survive. That's what the very clever Charles Dawkins has pointed out in his captivating book. But instead of "survival instinct," he has used the more pejorative appellation of "selfish desire." This has inspired some critics to violently attack Dawkins because his use of that term implies that there's not one scintilla of compassion in the human race. In response Dawkins has delightedly ripped these critics to shreds because they have accepted his implied *characterization* of the impulse without realizing that by attacking it they are attacking the very mechanism that drives evolution.

The natural instinct to survive only really becomes *selfish* in the usual pejorative sense when an individual puts his own survival above that of any other individual no matter what the situation. There are an incredible number of examples of humans doing just the opposite. But if you deliberately ignore the self awareness of individuals and consider only the supposed awareness of the inanimate gene, then you can imply that the gene deliberately forces some of the individual genes in its gene pool to sacrifice themselves in the interest of the survival of the pool, itself. In other words, Dawkins has satisfied the desire of determinists to claim that individuals have no free will and that their self awareness is an illusion by assigning self awareness and free will to the inanimate genes instead!

But if we accept *where* Dawkins has led us with his animated, self-aware gene as a reflection of the true nature of reality, then when Darwin's theory corrects this scenario by exposing the actual mechanism that drives evolution, it implies that nature, itself, causes those genes to survive which best suit its design—a design imbedded in the very nature of the universe.

Combine this with my contention that individuals do, indeed, have self-awareness and free will, then those individuals who sacrifice themselves out of love for their fellow human beings—*despite their very real, natural, gene-driven instinct for self-survival*—are probably accomplishing the purpose of whatever entity created the universe.

Does this mean that the creationists are correct? Unfortunately for them, the answer is "No." If creationists want to claim that there is a divine design to the universe that doesn't conflict with the revelations of science, then they must accept the overwhelming evidence that species gradually mutate. As I said, that's a fact, not a theory. And if they accept gradual mutation, then they must accept the fact that biblical scripture is wrong because it says that God created each living entity perfectly and immutably just as we see it now on Earth. The only way they can propose that God imbedded a purpose in the design of the universe is to accept the overwhelming evidence of gradual mutations which resulted in us. And the only theory that explains that gradualism in a way that is acceptable to scientists around the world is the one proposed by Darwin and Wallace.

And What About Christianity?

If what we have outlined here in this chapter is true—and the evidence is overwhelming that it is—then the claims of Christianity that Jesus was God Incarnate who came to redeem us for our sins can't be supported by the facts because there is no "fall from grace" in the process of gradual mutation. If Jesus of Nazareth didn't die on the cross to redeem a humanity that never "fell" in the first place, who was he and what did he really say and do 2000 years ago? The next chapter will show what biblical scholars are saying about the historical Jesus they see as they peer behind the Gospel wall created by the Christianizing scribes intent on "correcting' the gospel record.

Chapter 4

The Man Behind the Gospel Wall

I not only can't accept the Christian notion that Jesus was the Son of God, I can't believe that Jesus thought so either. Even if in later life he thought he might be the Messiah predicted in scripture, there was no reason why he would equate that with God since the Jewish scriptures never claimed that the Messiah would be the human equivalent of God Almighty. Nor did they talk of a "suffering Messiah," a later interpretation imposed on the Hebrew scriptures by Christians seeking to explain Jesus' crucifixion..

According to the only records we have of him, Jesus is portrayed as one of the most extraordinary humans in recorded history. I find it hard to disagree with that assessment. Jesus apparently performed healing miracles that were astonishing, and he spoke of spiritual things with a profound insight that could hardly be expected from an unlettered carpenter and laborer. Even his family and neighbors could hardly believe he was the same man they knew when he was growing up. And in addition he was born into an age and a society that expected events of monumental importance to be brought about by a God that had deliberately selected them as His chosen people. That fact led Jesus and his followers to attach a special significance to his remarkable transformation.

Was Jesus the Messiah who was to lead these chosen people from the bondage of the Roman occupation to God's Kingdom on earth, just as Moses had led the people out of Egypt to the promised land? History has proven that that wasn't the case because the Jews were not delivered from bondage and the apocalyptic Kingdom never appeared. But was his intention only to usher in a different kind of Kingdom, one that affected the spirit of mankind rather than its physical destiny?

The orthodox churches—Eastern and Western, Catholic and Protestant—claim that after he was tortured and killed, he rose from the dead in his human body, proving that he was the Son of God and identical with God Almighty even though his death and resurrection did not bring about the end of the world. He, himself, claimed that he was the Son of Man, and in the first three Gospels of the New Testament he never deviated from that self-description. Others have called him a prophet like Elijah, and still others have called him a self-deceived fraud.

I believe that he was something a great deal more than any of those assessments.

To answer the question of who Jesus really was, we have had to examine the validity of the contention that Jesus died to atone for mankind's sin and fall from grace. As we have seen from the previous chapter, the fossil record indicates that the literal Adam and Eve story can't be supported by the evidence. Once that's established, the entire theology of orthodox Christianity comes into question. Even if the Adam and Eve story is a mythological account of a real expulsion of our species of *Homo sapiens sapiens* because they exhibited an intelligence that freaked out the other members of their less mentally-gifted tribe, the idea that humanity's condition in life is a result of its basically evil nature is unsupportable. There is no fall from grace involved in the physical evolution of mankind. But if that's the case, what can we say then about the life and ministry of Jesus—the man behind the Gospel wall?

The only record we have of Jesus's life and teachings are in the canonical Gospels, several fragments of other early gospels, and the more recently discovered Gospel of Thomas and the so-called Gnostic texts unearthed at Nag Hammadi in Egypt in 1945. But before we consider these new texts, we must examine the more traditional accounts of Jesus's life and ministry.

The Canonical Gospels

While many would admit that Christianity is unique in many ways, a significant uniqueness that few really think about is the fact that it is the only religion that has at least four different officially recognized accounts about his life supposedly by people who actually knew him. No other religion has those kinds of sources available to it. For that reason many have attempted to reconstruct a more accurate account of what Jesus said and did by comparing both the similarities and contradictions among them.

There can be little doubt that the Gospel stories are talking about a real Jesus and his ministry,[1] but there were so many years between the actual event and the time when it was written down, and there are so many different versions of the same event, that it's hard to tell what exactly happened. It's as if the real historical Jesus is hidden behind a wall of conflicting evidence about his life and sayings. Many church-going Christians would disagree with that assessment, but careful analysis of the scriptures has led biblical scholars to wonder how much Jesus was "Christianized" by later Christian communities. As Paula Fredriksen, Professor of Scripture at Boston University School of Theology, says, "too many generations of pious copyists, anxious to 'correct' what to them might have seemed like defective recensions, stood between the first Christians and their modern readers."[2] However, there are some things about which modern scholars are pretty much in agreement.

---

[1] Although some have attempted to maintain that Jesus was a fictitious figure, few scholars give credence to such a silly notion. World-wide movements do not arise from illiterate peasants generating complex myths out of thin air.

[2] Fredriksen, Paula; *Who He Was*; http://www.tnr.com/101501/fredriksen101501_print.html.

According to Luke 3:23, Jesus was about 30 years old when he was crucified. After his crucifixion, nothing was written about him until Paul wrote his letters in 50 or 52 C.E., approximately 20 years after Jesus' death. Another 20 years passed before the first canonical gospel was written after the Jewish revolt against the Romans resulted in the destruction of the second Temple.[3] In the mean time it is obvious that stories about what Jesus said and did were told and retold among the faithful, and it is from this oral tradition that the later written Gospels were compiled.

Most scholars believe that Mark was written about the year 70 C.E., and that the author wrote for a community that was deeply disturbed by the destruction of the Temple during the initial Jewish revolt against the Romans. Matthew's emphasis on the Jewish origins of Jesus suggests that he was a Jew writing for a Jewish Christian community in conflict with the Pharisaic Judaism that dominated Jewish life in 85 C.E., more than a decade after the revolt. The author of Luke is thought to be addressing the later predominantly Gentile communities between 85 and 95 C.E. These three gospels are called the *Synoptic Gospels* because they roughly agree on the chronology of Jesus' ministry and they generally see things in the same way. John's Gospel on the other hand, which was probably written between 90 and 100 C.E., is totally different in tone and chronology, telling of two or more trips to Jerusalem instead of only one and placing the cleansing of the Temple in the first earliest trip, probably two years before his crucifixion. John also depicts an openly confrontational Jesus who proclaims his God-like nature[4] to any and all who would listen, a totally different Jesus from the secretive, almost self-effacing Son of Man[5] portrayed in the Synoptic Gospels.

All the earliest books of the New Testament that are available to us are written in Greek, not Aramaic, the language probably spoken by the Jews in Galilee at the time of Jesus's ministry. However, this has allowed scholars to determine some rather interesting things about some of the texts. For instance if the text of a passage found in one Gospel is repeated almost word for word in the Greek text of another, there can be little doubt that one was copied from the other since a transcription of different oral Aramaic traditions by two different translators would contain alternate phrasing. In both Matthew and Luke such passages can be found which are either identical or almost identical to ones found in Mark. Luke contains about half of Mark while Matthew includes almost all of it, and the length of each of their Gospels is almost twice as long as Mark's. This implies that Mark

---

[3] The first Temple, known as Solomon's Temple, existed from the 10th Century B.C.E. to 586 B.C.E. when it was destroyed by the Babylonians. The Second Temple, a reconstruction of the first, was completed in 515 B.C.E. and was extensively renovated by Herod in 35 C.E. It was destroyed by the Romans in 70 C.E..

[4] Cf. John 8:58, "Jesus said to them, Most assuredly, I tell you, before Abraham came into existence, I AM."

[5] Cf. Mark 8:30, "He charged them that they should tell no one about him."

was written earlier than the other two Gospels and was used by them as a major source for their stories.[6] In addition, since there are identical passages in Matthew and Luke which are not found in Mark, many scholars assume that another Greek source was available to them, as well. This is called the *Q* document, for the German word *Quelle* meaning *source*, and is what is known as a "sayings" gospel since all the passages are records of what Jesus said and contain no narratives about his life or descriptions of how he died.

So the first thing scholars have to do is decide which stories are of events which actually happened. For example, Matthew and Luke talk of a virgin birth while Mark and John's Gospels, and Paul's epistles, never mention such an astonishing event.[7] This is also true of the story about the resurrection of Lazarus which only appears in John. The Jesus depicted in Mark seems hostile to Jewish law while Matthew quotes Jesus as saying that he came to fulfill the law, not abolish it (Matt. 5:17). Even the 17th century biblical scholars who produced the King James version of the Bible indicated that the resurrections stories in Mark 16:9 – 20 were added later to the original Mark 16:8 "empty tomb" ending by putting them in italic and noting that they were later additions not found in the earliest scrolls and obviously not written by the same author. And while the Synoptic Gospels set the cleansing of the Temple just before Jesus' crucifixion, the Gospel of John said he did it very early in his ministry, no doubt to avoid the implication that it may have been a major reason for his execution. In fact, all of John sounds like a polemic written to justify the Christology of the early church. As Paula Fredriksen says, scholars have to find ways to interpret these conflicting texts and decide whether to combine them in some sort of harmony or acknowledge the contradiction and support one tradition over another.

For instance, practically all biblical scholars agree that the story about Jesus's baptism by John the Baptizer was undoubtedly a real event, primarily because it was such an obvious embarrassment to the Christian church. Even the addition of doves descending from heaven and divine voice-overs proclaiming this man to be the Son of God can't totally eliminate the strange idea that this divine being had to have his sins washed away in baptism. In the minds of a first-century community, this also put Jesus in a subservient position to John, in essence proclaiming that John was Jesus' mentor. This brings us to a crucial question in analyzing the New Testament scriptures.

---

[6] A few scholars have claimed that Mark extracted his shorter gospel from either Matthew or Luke rather than the other way around, but this seems counter intuitive. Someone who wanted to tell about a miraculous person like Jesus would add as many stories about him as possible, not eliminate them. In addition, Mark is the most primitive account of the four, writing as a person would who had very little writing experience in contrast to the other Gospels.

[7] And when you come right down to it, Matthew and Luke give totally contradictory accounts of the same event. Which do you pick?

The Problem of the Kingdom of God

Since there is no question that John the Baptizer proclaimed that the Kingdom of God was at hand and that all should repent, it isn't too much of a stretch to assume that Jesus thought the same thing. Indeed, in many passages Jesus proclaims that the Kingdom of God is near, but that only God knows when it will appear. But now the question is, does that mean that he thought that the end of the world—a physical apocalypse bringing about the "end of time"—was about to happen, or was he saying that he had already introduced the Kingdom? It seems apparent that John the Baptizer was convinced that a physical apocalypse was about to take place. That's why John was calling on the people to repent and to wash away their sins through baptism to prepare for its coming. But did Jesus hold the same view?

We will see that a great deal hangs on this question. For if Jesus predicted that the end of the world was coming before his generation[8] passed away—before the people to whom he was talking died—he was obviously wrong, which casts a great deal of doubt on his God-like nature and on the entire Christology of the church.

This has become known as the eschatological problem—the problem arising from (literally) "the study of end (or last) things." Eschatology is associated with the belief that Jesus thought the end of the world would come during or soon after his death. This makes his radical ethics proclaimed in the gospels a formula for anyone wishing to enter the Kingdom in the very near future. "Turning the other cheek" and "loving one's enemies as oneself" become readily achievable if one has to do it only for a few days, weeks, or months before getting one's reward.

As we have noted, Jesus proclaims in all three of the Synoptic Gospels that "this generation" will not pass away before the Kingdom of God arrives. The reason *immediacy statements* of this type were still included in a Gospel as late as Luke's is that they either imply or state explicitly that *some* of those listening to his voice would live to see the Kingdom appear. Even though Luke was written approximately 50 or 60 years after the death of Jesus, there could have been some who were still alive who had heard him say this.

The Gospel of John doesn't include such a statement because by the time John was written the expectation of an immanent Kingdom was fading away. He might have believed in a Kingdom of God,[9] but apocalypse was not the message that John wanted to convey. Rather, it was Jesus as the sacrificial lamb (John 1:29): "...he saw Jesus coming toward

---

[8] See Mark 9:1, "And he said to them, 'Truly, I say to you, there are some standing here who will not taste death before they see that the kingdom of God has come with power.'" See also Mark 13:30, Matt. 16:28; 24:34, and Luke 9:27;21:32-33.
[9] See John 3:3 and 3:5.

him, and said, 'Behold the Lamb of God who takes away the sins of the world.'"

Now it has been said that perhaps the only reason the *immediacy statements* were included in all three synoptic gospels was because the authors of Matthew and Luke copied Mark and just included them even though they may only have appeared initially in that one source. So you can't say that the score is three to one that Jesus actually said it, but that it's just even odds whether he did or didn't.

The problem with this is that the other synoptic authors didn't blindly copy everything that Mark said but modified many of his statements to fit their own traditions of what took place. For example in Mark 16:5-8, after the crucifixion when they came to the empty tomb, Mary Magdalene, Mary the mother of James, and Salome found " a young man…dressed in white" and "they said nothing to any one, for they were afraid." As we have noted, even the 17th Century scholars said that Mark ended his account there—no angels, no resurrection stories, and no mentioning of the event to the disciples at that time. Matthew 28:2-8 said just the two Marys saw "an angel of the Lord descended from heaven" and "with fear and great joy…ran to tell his disciples. And behold, Jesus met them and said, 'Hail!'" Luke 24:4-11 says that the two Marys and someone called Joanna saw not one but "two men…in dazzling apparel" and "returning from the tomb they told all this to the eleven and to all the rest…but these words seemed to them an idle tale, and they did not believe them."

None of these three accounts agree, even when it comes to something as simple and seemingly straight forward as the way the empty tomb was discovered. If Matthew and Luke had no difficulty in changing and adding to Mark's text to fit in with their own community's tradition of what happened at the tomb, why didn't they change or eliminate the *immediacy statements* if they weren't part of that same tradition? This implies that the score is still three to one that Jesus actually made these statements, because as time passed and the faithful died, these statements posed the same kind of embarrassment for the Christian community as the baptism by John.

Paul's Contribution

This is clearly brought out in Paul's first letter to the Corinthians. Apparently some Christians in Corinth thought that the faithful who had, as Paul euphemistically put it, "fallen asleep" would not partake of the Kingdom of God. Only those who would still be alive at that time would enter the Kingdom. But Paul holds that if one doesn't believe in the resurrection of the faithful from the dead, then one can't believe in the resurrection of Jesus. He says in First Corinthians 15:12-18,

> Now if Christ is preached, that he has been raised from
> the dead, how do some among you say that there is no

resurrection of the dead? But if there is no resurrection of the dead, neither has Christ been raised. If Christ has not been raised, then our preaching is in vain, and your faith also is in vain. Yes, we are found false witnesses of God, because we testified about God that he raised up Christ, whom he didn't raise up, if it is so that the dead are not raised. For if the dead aren't raised, neither has Christ been raised. If Christ has not been raised, your faith is vain; you are still in your sins. Then they also who are fallen asleep in Christ have perished. [10]

The very fact that Paul had to address this problem proves that both Paul and the Corinthians thought that the Kingdom was coming within their life times since they were obviously concerned that the faithful who had died would not participate in it. Why would they think that the Kingdom was immanent unless they were convinced that Jesus had said that it was?

Some have said that with this one paragraph Paul guaranteed the continuation of the Christian church. It has inspired others to claim facetiously that Christianity could have survived without Jesus, but definitely not without Paul! Perhaps that's overstating it a bit, but by implying that all the dead, past and future, are going to be resurrected when Christ comes back in Messianic glory, Paul successfully explains away why the faithful were dying before the expected Kingdom had arrived. And for 2000 years the expectation of the Parousia, Christ's Second Coming, has never disappeared from the liturgy of the Christian church because of this theological concept that there will be a mass resurrection and judgment of all humanity in the last days.

In other words, the Pauline concept of the Kingdom of God *seems* to be an apocalyptic one in which the world as we know it is destroyed and a new Messianic Kingdom is established on earth. However, nothing about Paul's theology is as simple as all that. For Paul, those who believed in Christ, and especially in his death and resurrection, have already died and been reborn "in Christ," as represented by their baptism and partaking of the bread and wine in the communion service. As he says in Romans 6:3-5:

> ...don't you know that all we who were baptized into Christ Jesus were baptized into his death? We were buried therefore with him through baptism to death, that just like Christ was raised from the dead through the glory of the Father, so we also might walk in newness of life. For if we have become united with him in the

---

[10] A peculiar "backward" proof. Since they believed Christ was raised from the dead, their experience of thousands of years that no one is ever raised from the dead must of necessity be wrong. It's like a would-be inventor I once knew who replied when he was told that his idea for an amazing flying machine violated Newton's laws of motion that Newton's laws of motion must be wrong!

> likeness of his death, we will also be part of his resurrection...

Thus the faithful have already entered a kind of spiritual Kingdom which will be reaffirmed when "the dead shall be raised up incorruptible, and we will all be changed" (I Cor. 15:52) to live eternally in the coming (physical) Messianic Kingdom. So it seems as if Paul is saying that there are two Kingdoms of God—one which occurs within us when we are "baptized into Christ Jesus" and another which will occur at the end of time when the world will be destroyed and Christ will return to usher in the physical Kingdom of God.

As we have seen, this double concept of the Kingdom by Paul has led the Church to proclaim that Jesus did predict the apocalyptic end of the world. The question that must be answered, however, is whether Jesus thought it was going to happen in his generation. And even more importantly, did he actually think that if he brought about his own death, he could force the event to happen? That is the penultimate question that has been argued by some theologians from the 17th century to the present day. And no one has provided us with a more definitive history of this conflict than Albert Schweitzer (1875-1965) in his great work, *The Quest for the Historical Jesus.*

Schweitzer's Eschatology

George Santayana was supposedly the first to say that "those who ignore history are doomed to repeat it." As R. H. Lightfoot once remarked in conversation: "If those who pay lip-service to Schweitzer would only read him, half the unnecessary books which now get written about the New Testament would never see the light of day."[11]

Nowhere is this more apparent than in the current attempts to find out what Jesus really said and did by eliminating the supposedly later alterations by scribes. A big part of the problem is that if one *must* reconcile the real historical Jesus as revealed in a critical analysis of the scriptures with our modern conception of him as expressed in the Church, one is forced to eliminate certain statements in the text which imply that Jesus was not the Son of God. This is especially true of the eschatological statements, such as the ones we have called the *immediacy statements.* Schweitzer has effectively identified the problems of all the attempts made prior to the 20th century to ignore eschatology in the scriptures with an attention to detail that cannot be found in any other single popular account.

Modern theologians are no different from many whom Schweitzer considered. They can't accept the eschatological nature of Mark and Matthew without giving up their belief in Jesus as the Christ, the Son of God. That not only threatens their faith but also their reason for remaining

---

[11] Schweitzer, Albert; *The Quest for the Historical Jesus,* Edited by John Bowden; Fortress Press, Minneapolis; 2001, p. 488, footnote 3.

in their chosen professions. Nowhere is this more significantly demonstrated than in the actions of Schweitzer, himself, who left theology at the height of his career in 1913, returned to school to study medicine, and became a medical missionary to Africa. From that time until his death his theology consisted of a "reverence for life," not a reverence for Jesus as the Son of God. He was obviously a man of his convictions.

Schweitzer's eschatological claim is that Jesus thought, not only that the end of the world would occur in his lifetime, but that he would be the catalyst that would bring it about. At first Jesus set out to create the conditions that would convince God to bring in the Kingdom by sending out his disciples to all of Israel, preaching the Kingdom, healing the sick, and casting out demons. When that didn't work, he realized that something more drastic was needed. He himself, as the Son of Man, would usher in the Kingdom with his own death "on behalf of the many," taking the place of the suffering of the faithful as later Christians claimed was predicted in scripture.

To accomplish this end, he and his disciples set out for Jerusalem for the Passover, arriving in triumph as a conquering king into the city, causing a huge disturbance in the temple by overturning the money tables in sight of the Roman garrison (which could see directly into the courtyard of the temple), and proclaiming that a new Kingdom was about to be established on Earth. He is successful—the authorities seize him, whip him, and crucify him. But the end doesn't come as he thought it would while he was hanging on the cross. In the end, the two earliest gospels, Mark (15:34) and Matthew (27:46), report that he cried out in Aramaic, "Eloi, Eloi, [or Eli, Eli] lama sabachthani?" meaning, "My God, my God, why hast thou forsaken me?"[12] And in Mark, at least, the only sign of the arrival of the Kingdom was an empty tomb.

This, according to Schweitzer, is what the eschatological interpretation of the earliest Scriptures tells us about the historical Jesus. Once the primitive Church realized that the Kingdom was not coming immediately and that the world would not be destroyed, it concentrated on the spiritual Christ it saw in Jesus. As Schweitzer says:

> ...the world continued to exist, and its continuance brought this one-sided view to an end. The supra-mundane Christ and the historical Jesus of Nazareth had to be brought together into a single personality at once historical and raised above time. That was accomplished

---

[12] These are the opening words of the 22nd Psalm and are thought by the orthodox to have been uttered to show his disciples that the so-called prophecies of the suffering Messiah had been fulfilled. But if Jesus was attempting to force the coming of the Kingdom as we have postulated here, he would not have been quoting the Psalm to convince his followers that he was the suffering Messiah predicted in scripture but a plea to God, Himself, to bring in the Kingdom. The author of Luke must have thought so too since he left out this haunting Aramaic cry in his crucifixion story, even though he copied Mark extensively elsewhere.

by Gnosticism and the Logos Christology. Both, from opposite standpoints, because they were seeking the same goal, agreed in sublimating the historical Jesus into the supra-mundane Idea.[13]

In other words, the religion *of* Jesus became the religion *about* Jesus. The Logos Christology is represented in the Gospel of John and has its roots in the idea that Jesus was the sacrificial Lamb of God who took away the sins of humanity. Christian Gnosticism, on the other hand, is best represented by the Gospel of Thomas that never mentions the crucifixion. As Schweitzer says, both of these traditions are indifferent to the historical Jesus since the Gospel of John is more intent on emphasizing the divinity of Jesus as the Christ while Thomas takes the opposite approach by emphasizing the humanity of Jesus while proclaiming that all of humanity was really inherently divine.

Before we examine the Gospel of Thomas, however, it behooves us to take a careful look at the conclusions produced by another group of scholars, the Fellows of the Jesus Seminar, whose methodology is completely different from Schweitzer's.

The Non-Eschatology of the Jesus Seminar

Founded in 1985 by Robert W. Funk, former professor of the New Testament at the University of Montana, the Jesus Seminar meets semiannually and initially focused on the authenticity of Jesus' sayings in the four canonical gospels and the Gospel of Thomas. Originally composed of about 200 members, they now number 74, twenty of whom are acknowledged scholars in the field of the New Testament but only fourteen of whom have published.

Of the seven "pillars" or analytical methods which the members of the seminar used to get their results, the one which is of greatest interest for us is the fifth, which "liberates the non-eschatological Jesus" from Schweitzer's eschatology.[14] The other "pillars" need not concern us, but the fifth definitely limits the participants only to those who believe as Funk does that Jesus never thought the end of the world was about to happen. It isn't surprising then that all of Jesus' eschatological sayings are considered to be later additions made by the Christian communities and are eliminated.

The rational for this point of view is spelled out in *The Five Gospels* on pages 136, 137. After quoting the *immediacy statements* in Mark 13:30 and 9:1, they contrast them with Luke 17:21, "God's imperial rule is right there in your presence," and Luke 11:20, "But if by God's finger I drive out demons, then for you God's imperial rule has arrived."

---

[13] *Quest*, p. 4,5.
[14] *The Five Gospels: The Search for the Authentic Words of Jesus*; New Translation and Commentary by Robert W. Funk, Roy W. Hoover, and The Jesus Seminar; Macmillan Publishing Co., New York, 1993, p. 4.

The Fellows admit that "The texts cited...can be used to support either view"—namely that the apocalypse was immanent or that the Kingdom was already present. While the parables also support either view, the Fellows felt that "they did not reflect an apocalyptic view of history." The question is, can we really eliminate the sweeping, clearly stated *immediacy statements* while retaining the supposedly non-apocalyptic passages that merely hint at a Kingdom that Jesus has already established?

Perhaps even more serious is the effort the Fellows will eventually have to take to reconcile the letters of Paul to this non-eschatological Jesus. It is true that Paul never met Jesus and never heard him speak, but it is obvious that he believed that Jesus did predict that the Kingdom was going to arrive in Paul's lifetime. Even though he supplied the rationale that allowed the arrival of the apocalyptic Kingdom to be extended indefinitely by explaining how the recent death of believers would not exclude them from participating in it, there can be little doubt in reading the epistles that he believed it would still occur in the immediate future. And he believed this because that's what every one of the faithful knew that Jesus said. Remember, that was only 20 years after Jesus' ministry. Why assume people in Paul's time would have such poor memories that they would misquote such an important statement by Jesus that predicted the coming end of the world *in their lifetimes*?

The Methodology of the Jesus Seminar

The method the Fellows of the Seminar used to vote on whether they thought Jesus actually said what was recorded in a particular passage was to drop one of four colored beads into a voting box. Each color represented a different shading of opinion, ranging from red to black:

Red: Jesus really said this.

Pink: This sounds like something Jesus might have said, but we're not positive.

Gray: Jesus didn't really say this but it's similar to something he might say. Close but no cigar.

Black: Jesus didn't say this. It's a later addition reflecting the beliefs of a "Christian" community.

These were weighted as follows: Red—3, Pink—2, Gray—1, and Black—0. On each ballot the points were added up and divided by the number of Fellows voting. Once they were converted into percentages, it gave the Fellows the feeling that they were avoiding a yes or no vote since it allowed each one to shade his or her opinion giving it a more scholarly flavor. All the votes would count even though it was thought that black votes would carry more weight, just as students assumed happened when one "F" seemed to be exceptionally influential in pulling down an average. So the

Fellows of the Seminar concluded that this shortcoming was in keeping with their philosophy of "when in doubt, take it out."

They were wrong, of course. It may seem like an "F" will be unduly influential on a weighted average, but that's a psychological influence, not a statistical one. Statistically, it's no more influential than an "A." But this attitude is significant in that it reveals the bias of the Seminar Fellows to doubt most of the sayings.

By using this colored-bead voting technique, each Fellow could vote in secret so that no one could know who voted what. That's very democratic but it makes absolutely no sense in this situation. To illustrate the ridiculous nature of this technique, consider their evaluation of Mark 3:34: "Here are my mother and my brothers. Whoever does God's will, that's my brother and sister and mother." When the Fellows summed up the score, they found that "weighted averages...fell just on either side of the dividing line between pink and gray."[15] So even though that represented a 50-50 split in the vote, they made the saying gray, following their principle of when in doubt, take it out. Suppose a couple of the Fellows who had voted gray or black on the day of this vote had come down with a cold and didn't attend. Then the vote would have been pink.

In other words, two scholars sneeze and Jesus suddenly speaks! Now there's a scriptural exegesis that'll blow your mind. Needless to say, this demonstrates that neither science nor true scholarship are based on popular vote. If they were, we would still believe the Earth was the center of the universe and that Hitler's Diaries were real.

But the real shocker is that the Fellows could only find 18% of the sayings of Jesus to be authentic; i.e., either red or pink. In fact, in the Gospel of John, only one short sentence was considered authentic enough to give it a pink vote—namely, John 4:43, "A prophet gets no respect on his own turf."[16] All the rest of John is black except for another short gray sentence. I admit that I believe John is by far the least reliable of the four Gospels because of his obvious intention to portray Jesus as God Incarnate no matter how much he has to distort the Synoptic texts to do so. But this wholesale elimination of what Jesus says in John's Gospel points to the fallacy of the Seminar's technique. How on earth could they possibly deduce that *nothing* in John could be attributed directly to Jesus?

The answer is that they couldn't. The Gospels are, after all, the only sources that anyone has of what Jesus said and did during his lifetime, and there are many passages in John's Gospel that can also be found in similar words in the other Gospels. Because of this it was one of Schweitzer's criteria that as little violation of the text as possible was essential to glean any legitimate conclusions about the ideas and thoughts

---

[15] *Ibid*, p. 53.
[16] *Ibid*, p. 412. It implies that the Fellows accepted this quote because it explains away why Jesus's neighbors and relatives refused to believe that he was exceptional in any way.

of Jesus of Nazareth. Schweitzer was true to this principle, and while he concentrated primarily on Mark and Matthew as the earliest and therefore probably the most accurate of the four Gospels, he avoided attributing sayings to later additions on flimsy evidence or *a priori* assumptions. The Fellow's meat-axe approach to the texts violates this principle and brings all of their conclusions into doubt. But even when their conclusions are examined on their own, they are often questionable

Consider their analysis of the *immediacy statement* in Mark 49:1, "And he used to tell them, 'I swear to you: Some of those standing here won't ever taste death before they see God's imperial rule set in with power!'" The Fellows say that Mark's congregation thought that the arrival of the Kingdom was imminent. And "On these grounds a substantial number of Fellows found it necessary to attribute this formulation to Mark rather than to Jesus."[17]

Am I missing something here? Why in heaven's name would Mark add this "false" statement to his Gospel even though it doesn't advance any Christianizing agenda on the part of Mark or his community? After all, Mark's Gospel was written 40 years after Jesus' death and 20 years after Paul spoke of the faithful dying *without* experiencing the Kingdom. Things were already looking very shaky for the validity of this apocalyptic prediction so why include it?

Since the passage says that God's rule will be set in "with power," it is evident that the people in Mark, Matthew, and Luke's time thought the end of the world was coming. Where did they get that idea? John the Baptizer certainly thought that was the case, but the Fellows claim that Jesus didn't. So must we conclude that these communities thought John's prediction was more accurate than Jesus'? Or were the disciples so dense— or was Jesus so subtle—that they completely misinterpreted what he said? And when the Kingdom didn't come and didn't come and people were dying before there was any sign of it "coming with power," were Mark, Matthew, and Luke really so mindlessly stubborn that they insisted that the statement must be put into the gospel even though Jesus never said it. It makes no sense for them to include it when the failure of the Kingdom to appear to *any* of those who supposedly heard Jesus say this implied that Jesus didn't know what was going to happen and therefore was not an omniscient God.

This wholesale elimination of troubling passages is an extreme violation of the text. As Schweitzer reveals in his account of earlier attempts to find the historical Jesus, this "method" has been used countless times by people who wanted Scripture to support their own views on what *should* have happened so many years ago. It's neither scholarly nor honest. You can't take the only evidence you have and chop it up to conform to an *a priori* concept. If you do, you might as well chuck out the entire text and

---

[17] *Ibid*, p. 80.

substitute your own, which in a sense is exactly what the Jesus Seminar Fellows have done.

Critics of the Jesus Seminar have claimed that it is a blatant attempt to destroy Christianity by denying the virgin birth and the resurrection, but a closer reading of their results implies the opposite. By denying that Jesus said anything about an apocalypse occurring in "this generation's" life time, the Fellows are actually rescuing Jesus from his devastatingly wrong prediction. That has inspired at least one biblical expert to claim that Christianity has based itself on the most tawdry of religious figures—an unprophetic prophet—no different from the many prophets of doom who have littered the landscape over the last two millennia!

The Seminar's attempt to rewrite the gospels is nowhere more evident than in the fact that the removal of all references in Scripture to an apocalyptic Kingdom has contributed to the elimination of over 80% of the sayings of Jesus by the Jesus Seminar. That's unacceptable. But by the same token, if one were to eliminate or alter all passages which implied that the Kingdom was already present, another violation of the text would result, especially in the Gospel of Thomas. As we will see in the next section, the latter sheds a completely different light on the question of Jesus' divinity and the possibility of human transcendence.

The Gospel Of Thomas

The four gospels in the New Testament are so familiar to us that it's easy to assume that they were the only gospels written. In point of fact as one scholar put it, by the second century gospel writing had almost become a "cottage industry" as different Christian communities evolved and had their own oral traditions. Bishop Irenaeus of Lyon in 180 C.E. suggested that four was the proper number for the gospels because of the four corners of the earth, the four winds, and the four beasts of the apocalypse, not because there were only four available. A more rational reason might be that these four were selected to satisfy the majority of communities, each of whom had their own different traditions about the life and sayings of Jesus. This is why one should consider these four gospels as four alternative accounts about him and not four different aspects of the same story which have to be somehow reconciled.

In 1945 at a site near the Egyptian town of Nag Hammadi at the base of the mountain range Jabal al-Tarif in upper Egypt some peasant boys found 12 codices (books) containing supposedly Gnostic writings and gospels dating from the 3rd and 4th centuries (although the originals may have been as early as 70-140 C.E.). One of those gospels, the Gospel of

Thomas, contained only the sayings of Jesus and no narrative about his life and ministry.[18]

The discovery of this new gospel casts a very different light on the man behind the gospel wall. Elaine H. Pagels, Professor of religion at Princeton University, points out[19] that in the Gospel of Thomas Jesus admonishes the disciples to look within themselves for the Kingdom of God, not to the external world. Jesus is quoted in Thomas 108 as saying, "Whoever drinks from my mouth will become as I am, and I will become that person, and the mysteries will be revealed to him," a concept which is totally different from the utterly unique Jesus as Son of God depicted in the Gospel of John. In the Gospel of Thomas Jesus says we share the same natures. The Gospel claims that one must go on a spiritual search of one's own soul to discover that you're a child of God just like Jesus.

That certainly doesn't sound like the totally-other divine Christ of the last gospel and the letters of Paul.

These texts were unknown for almost 2000 years because they were condemned as heretical by orthodox Christians when the Church was struggling with various factions to define an "acceptable" doctrine of belief. Our old friend Bishop Irenaeus condemned Gnosticism as blasphemy and forced the suppression of all Gnostic literature. Up till 1945 almost all our knowledge of these texts was what the orthodox, like Irenaeus, said about these so-called heretical documents—not exactly the best source for reliable information about them. However, as Elaine Pagels says, "The campaign against heresy involved an involuntary admission of its persuasive power [even though] the bishops prevailed."[20]

The *gnosis* in Gnosticism means *knowledge*, not in the logical sense but rather as intuition, such as in *knowing* oneself. "And to know oneself, they claimed, is to know human nature and human destiny...Yet to know oneself, at the deepest level, is simultaneously to know God; this is the secret of *gnosis*."[21]

Gnosticism existed long before the time of Jesus. It traditionally held that the world was made by an evil lesser god, a Demiurge, that trapped our pure spirits in evil bodies. The purpose of the gnosis was to liberate us from our bodies so that we could join with the spiritual God who was superior to the Demiurge. It is unclear how many of these older Gnostic traditions were incorporated into the Christian version of Gnosticism, but the recently discovered Gospel of Judas (cf., later in this chapter) explicitly incorporates them while the Gospel of Thomas only implies a connection.

---

[18] Lending validity to the possibility that another sayings gospel, the Q document, may well have existed at one time.

[19] Pagels, Elaine H.; *The Gnostic Gospels*, Vintage Books, A Division of Random House, Inc.; New York; 1979.

[20] *Ibid*, p. xviii.

[21] *Ibid*, p. xix.

One can see how the idea of an internal Kingdom would appeal to people looking for an alternative to the failed apocalyptic *immediacy statements* of Jesus found in the Synoptic Gospels. But instead of transforming Jesus into the Christ—the totally "other," the transcendent Son of God found throughout the Gospel of John—this version of Christian Gnosticism transforms us into Jesus! That's why in Thomas there is no narrative of the life of Jesus but a collection of his sayings that emphasize this internalization of the Kingdom of God. The resurrection stories are incorporated only when the orthodox want to elevate Jesus to godhood in order to explain away the shameful nature of Jesus' crucifixion as a common criminal and convert it into the divine redemption of the basic sinful status of humanity. In Gnosticism, Jesus would never be resurrected and come back to this evil world of the Demiurge, because crucifixion was his escape to the realm of the true spiritual God.

But if Gnosticism was so attractive, why didn't it become dominant rather than the so-called orthodox faith? Part of the answer lies in the structure of the Church, itself. Orthodoxy lends itself to a hierarchical order in the Church with the Trinity at the top and humanity at the bottom. That makes bishops, priests, and deacons fit in nicely between the two. Gnosticism on the other hand is anarchical in nature. Each human is his own conduit to God. As Thomas quotes Jesus in verse 70, "If you bring forth what is within you, what you bring forth will save you. If you do not bring forth what is within you, what you do not bring forth will destroy you." A bishop has no more right to tell you what the will of God is than your next-door neighbor, because all you need to do is to look into your own soul.

But as a hierarchical dictatorship, the Church is far more stable and structurally coherent than a confederation of individuals and is much more likely to survive as a self-contained entity. In any case, its power over groups of individuals is considerably stronger and more likely to dominate the latter than the other way around. It isn't so much that the orthodox *belief* is more acceptable and valid than the Gnostic, but that the organization it leads to is more apt to survive. The surprising thing is that even after Gnosticism was supposedly safely tucked away as a heresy, the idea of a Jesus who was not God's equal should so persistently reappear, even as late as the 4th Century during the reign of Constantine.

Constantine and the Arian Heresy

By the 3rd Century the Roman Empire was beginning to come unglued—wanting to become Emperor was equivalent to having a death wish. When Diocletian came to power in 282 C.E., he attempted to break the chain of assassinations by sharing the rule of the Empire with Maximian, a capable general Diocletian evidently trusted. Maximian controlled the West while Diocletian ruled the East. Each ruler (called an "Augustus") chose a successor (called a "Caesar"). As Will Durant puts it:

Each Augustus pledged himself to retire after twenty years in favor of his Caesar, who would then appoint a "Caesar" to aid and succeed him in turn. Each Augustus gave his daughter in marriage to his "Caesar," adding the ties of blood to those of law. In this way, Diocletian hoped, wars of succession would be avoided, government would recapture continuity and authority, and the Empire would stand on guard at four strategic points against internal rebellion and external attack. It was a brilliant arrangement, which had every virtue but unity and freedom.[22]

Diocletian chose Byzantium, which eventually became Constantinople, as his capital rather than Rome. All four men ruled from different capitals, but "Each law of each ruler was issued in the name of all four, and was valid for the realm."[23] The resulting 23 years of peace was achieved at the cost of establishing a giant bureaucracy and a controlled economy that eventually collapsed and brought about the abdication of both Diocletian and Maximian in the year 305. The two Caesars, Galerius and Constantius Chlorus, became the new *Augusti* of the East and West, and almost immediately civil war broke out. Diocletian's formula of two *Augusti* and two Caesars quickly degenerated into four *Augusti* (plus two more pretenders to the throne) since no one wanted the subservient position of Caesar. One of these *Augusti* was Constantine, son of Constantius Chlorus.

Constantine proved to be a talented general and eventually met the army of Maxentius, *Augustus* of the West, at a town nine miles north of Rome near the Tiber river. In the afternoon before the battle he supposedly saw a flaming cross in the sky with the words "in this sign conquer" written in Greek, and that night dreamt he heard a voice commanding him to paint the Christian symbol on the shields of his men. His victory the next day at the Battle of the Milvian Bridge secured his place in history as the first Christian ruler of the Holy Roman Empire.

Whether Constantine was a truly committed Christian or simply a clever politician who took advantage of a fast-growing and autonomous organization to stabilize his vast empire is open to question.[24] In any case he soon discovered that the Christian community was not quite as autonomous as he originally thought. Violent controversies immediately broke out between sections of the Church, the most serious being the one over the Arian question of *consubstantiality*.

Arius was a humble priest in the Egyptian town of Baucalis who started to preach in 318 C.E. that Christ was created by God "in time," was

---

[22] Durant, Will; *The Story of Civilization: Part III; Caesar and Christ*; Simon and Schuster, New York, 1944, p. 640.
[23] *Ibid.*
[24] He only consented to be baptized on his death bed.

therefore not coeternal with him, and was simply the highest of all created beings, created by God out of nothing. He was therefore not *consubstantial* with the Father.

The Arians put up some pretty good arguments since there are surprising number of passages that strongly imply that Jesus talked about God as if He were a separate entity. For example he prays to God to save him before the Romans came to arrest him in the garden. Even the Gospel of John indicates this separation when he quotes Jesus as saying in 5:30, "I don't seek my own will, but the will of my Father who sent me." And how could he claim that God was greater than he if he didn't mean it.

In addition, even though they thought Jesus was less than the Father, the Arians felt there was no reason to hold that humanity's sins could not have been forgiven by his crucifixion because the Father created the Christ as his Son for the purpose of redeeming humanity. Jesus also says, "I can do nothing on my own authority" but only as the Father dictates. And as we have seen, in the eyes of the populace of this age that meant that Jesus was even more powerful in his relationship with God than a Caesar was to his Augustus even though a Caesar had much more authority than an ordinary citizen. Jesus was a perfect representative of God without being Him just as a portrait can perfectly represent a man without being the man.

The rapid spread of this view within the clergy alarmed Bishop Alexander who ordered a council of Egyptian bishops to condemn this doctrine as heretical. Since many had already accepted Arian's proposition, the controversy grew heated causing Constantine to call the first ecumenical council at Nicaea to resolve the issue. Athanasius, an archdeacon under Alexander, was the most vehemently opposed to Arius and claimed that denying Christ's consubstantiation (*homoousia*) with God opened the door to polytheism, and although it was difficult to comprehend the orthodox doctrine of the Trinity—that three distinct persons could exist within God— he maintained that it was a mystery that had to be accepted on faith. All but 17 of the 318 bishops present agreed and issued a statement which eventually became the Nicene Creed recited in many services to this day. The Arians agreed to sign the document if they could substitute a Greek "i", the *iota*, to the key word making it *homoiousia* or "like" God instead of *homoousia,* "identical" to God.[25] The majority refused and Constantine put his imprimatur on the document, making it the law of the land.

But if Constantine thought this solved the controversy, he was sadly mistaken. Even he, himself, changed his mind about the Arians at

·

---

[25] This is where the expression, "It doesn't make an *iota* of difference," came from. This *iota* resulted in bloody street fights that caused more deaths than all those from the previous two centuries of persecution.

least twice during the rest of his reign.[26] Bishops were lynched by street mobs as the fortunes of one side or the other gained sway. When Constantine's son, Constantius, gained the throne, he intensified the nature of the conflict.

> Constantius took theology more seriously than his father. He made his own inquiry into the paternity of Jesus, adopted the Arian view, and felt a moral obligation to enforce it upon all Christendom. Athanasius, who had returned to his see[27] after Constantine's death, was again expelled (339 C.E.); church councils, called and dominated by the new Emperor, affirmed merely the likeness, not the consubstantiality, of Christ with the Father; ecclesiastics loyal to the Nicene Creed were removed from their churches, sometimes by the violence of the mobs; for half a century it seemed that Christianity would be Unitarian and abandon the divinity of Christ.[28]

Athanasius, a stubborn and forceful personality, stuck by his guns, and even though he had to flee his see five times in fear for his life, he never faltered in his belief that Jesus was God incarnate. For the 50 years from 323 to 373 C.E. he suffered for that belief during the vacillations of Constantine and the disfavor of Constantius. When he persuaded Pope Julius I to restore him to his see in 340, riots broke out in Alexandria when the Eastern bishops denied the Pope's jurisdiction in the city and installed an Arian in his place. It was during the following year from 342 to 343 that civil strife resulted in the death of thousands on both sides.

Not an auspicious beginning for the establishment of the divinity of Jesus throughout the rest of Church history. Indeed, if the Arians had been a little more pugnacious than the orthodox mobs, if Athanasius had been less stubborn and persuasive, or if Arius had been a bishop instead of a lowly priest, belief in Jesus as God Almighty today could well be the heresy and not Arianism. The amazing thing is that the Arian viewpoint could have spread so rapidly in such a short amount of time and that it became an almost equal contender for the accepted dogma of the Church. Much as today's orthodox Christians might wish to think that the outcome was inevitable, it was actually a very close call and could easily have gone the other way.

---

[26] And although he was ambivalent about the whole question even at the end of his life, he was baptized on his death bed by Eusebius, an Arian Bishop of Nicomedia.

[27] A bishop's "see" is the place or seat of authority from which he rules his diocese.

[28] Durant, Will; *The Story of Civilization: Part IV; The Age of Faith*; Simon and Schuster, New York, 1950, p. 8.

And Then There Are the Resurrection Stories

It is interesting to note that the crucifixion is the one story that all four of the canonical gospels agree upon in the greatest detail.[29] But when we come to the resurrection stories, none of the stories are the same. Only the empty tomb is present in all four, and as we have seen, even the details of how that discovery was made are totally different.

What is interesting about all of these stories is that in most of them Jesus is seldom recognized—only later do they "realize" that they had been talking to the risen Christ. Sometimes a group of disciples come upon Jesus but only some of them recognize him. For example, consider Matt. 28:17: "When they saw him, they bowed down to him, but some doubted." If all the disciples saw him, how could some doubt it? What did they doubt—that the person the others were bowing to was really Jesus, or didn't they see what the others saw? If it was really Jesus in his restored body—a man many had been living with for many days—how could they not recognize him?

Other resurrection stories are very obviously ones in which people talk themselves into believing that they actually saw and spoke with the risen Jesus. Consider the one in Luke 24:13-32 where the two disciples on the road to Emmaus encounter a man they don't recognize, walk and converse with him for a considerable distance, and then finally "recognize" him when he breaks bread and then disappears from their sight. The charming thing about this story is that they admit that they talked themselves into believing that they knew it was him all along. But if it had really been Jesus, why didn't they recognize him immediately and why would he disappear right after revealing himself to them? What would have been the point of the revelation? Although we don't really know what actually happened, we can speculate that the act of the breaking of bread, the most emotional and significant action of Jesus just before his crucifixion, would trigger all kinds of emotions in those who had witnessed it at the Last Supper. Is it too much of a stretch of the imagination to suppose that while witnessing that action once again they would flash on the image of Jesus doing the same thing? And couldn't their reaction be startling enough to the stranger to prompt him to make a hasty retreat? This passage is an excellent example of the overwhelming desire of the disciples to believe that their beloved Jesus was still with them by remembering ordinary events as miraculous encounters with his risen presence.

Then we have the encounter in John 21:4 when "Jesus stood on the beach, yet the disciples didn't know that it was Jesus." He tells them to cast their nets at a particular spot and they pull up a big load of fish, a supposedly miraculous event because they had been unable to find any fish

---

[29] Although in John's Gospel Jesus is crucified on the day before the Passover meal when the lambs are sacrificed and not the day after as in the Synoptic Gospels. Can you guess why?

up to that point. But a modern Galilean fisherman says that this is the way they have fished in this area for centuries. A lookout stands on the shore and can see where the schools of fish are, which the men in the boats can't see from their perspective. He then shouts to them where to cast their nets. The technique has obviously worked for over 2000 years without the necessity of a miracle.

Jesus then invites his bemused disciples to breakfast with him, but "none of the disciples dared inquire of him, 'Who are you?' knowing that it was the Lord"(John 21:12). In other words, they really didn't *know* it was Jesus, but sort of guessed it was him, even though they had lived with him day after day for months. Very strange.

In point of fact, these types of stories reveal the kind of strain the witnesses were under to convince their listeners that they actually had seen the resurrected Jesus. With the empty tomb there had to be some way to account for the missing body. When the followers reported that they had seen Jesus, it was natural to assume that they had seen him physically, so ordinary encounters with strangers or spiritual visions became physical encounters with a risen Jesus. It is also interesting to note that the later the Gospel was written the more physical the descriptions become until in Luke 24:39 and John 20:20 the resurrected Jesus eats some food and encourages his disciples to touch his wounds.

And speaking of John, it's also notable that his is the only Gospel that told of the guard piercing Jesus's side with a spear. Apparently, there were skeptics in the Gospel writer's time who were suggesting that perhaps Jesus was still alive when he was taken down from the cross since it was normally the Roman's lovely practice to break the legs of the crucified to cause or make sure of their death, and that obviously didn't happen to Jesus. By having a soldier pierce his side, it explained why Jesus was indeed killed but was still able to walk around on sound legs after his bodily resurrection from the dead even though he had suffered a Roman crucifixion. And since John's Gospel goes on to insist that "He who has seen has testified, and his testimony is true. He knows that he tells the truth, that you may believe"(John 19:35), it makes one wonder if the writer wasn't protesting a bit too much to offset this interesting argument by his contemporary skeptics.

Oddly enough, even though great emphasis is put on Jesus' *bodily* resurrection to coincide with the empty tomb, sometimes the Gospel authors have him appearing out of thin air, and in the case of John, in a room carefully described as shut and presumably locked "for fear of the Jews!" Jesus has his own physical body, but it's really a spiritual body because it can pass through closed doors and suddenly appear. It seems as if the gospel writers are trying to have it both ways, but logically they can't. To say that his body can be both a non-physical spirit and a physical body at the same time is not only logically impossible, it contradicts the original claim that Jesus died and was resurrected in his formerly living, totally material body that was buried in the tomb.

And finally we come back to the primary problem with the resurrection stories—they aren't anywhere near alike. Many of the earlier accounts of Jesus's life in the Synoptic Gospels were different versions of the same story. Here, the stories aren't even remotely related to one another. If all four Gospels can't agree on any of these spectacular accounts of Jesus' physical reappearance, the significance of the accounts themselves must be questioned.

Applying 21st Century Science to the Nature Miracles

Before the 17th century it was easy to accept the claim that Jesus was bodily "lifted up to heaven" because everybody *knew* that heaven existed just on the other side of that sphere of stars rotating around our stationary flat earth. But as Joseph Campbell pointed out, we now know that if he was bodily lifted up, he would still be in our galaxy less than 2000 light-years away because nothing physical can travel faster than the speed of light!

Now before you claim that that's just a rather facetious observation, it's important to realize that it reveals a truth that must be dealt with. It goes without saying that we know a lot more about the physical universe than early-century peasants and scribes. But it's incumbent upon us to ask some rather devastating questions about certain claims made in the Bible in light of that advanced knowledge.

For example, if Jesus was really born of a virgin, what did his DNA look like? We now know that all life forms on Earth contain blueprints (or more accurately, recipes) of their nature in DNA which contains four different types of nucleotides: adenine, guanine, cytosine, and thiamine. If Jesus didn't have human DNA, then Jesus was not a human but either another type of physical being or a pure spirit. If you believe the former, then Jesus wasn't God incarnate in human form or any other type of life form found on Earth. If you believe Jesus was pure spirit, that would make you a Docetist; namely, one who thinks Jesus only appeared to have a body and was not really a physical man. Unfortunately, Docetism was condemned by the Christian church at the council of Chalcedon in 451, so that would make you a heretic. Or you could claim that God used something like parthenogenesis in which an animal, like certain lizards, can reproduce without sex. The only problem with that is that parthenogenesis wouldn't produce a male Jesus but only a clone of Mary since the resulting offspring would contain just her DNA alone.

If the spiritual nature of Jesus was due to the type of DNA he possessed, then modern molecular manipulation techniques could presumably eventually produce another God-Incarnated human once the correct pattern was discovered. After all, out of the billions upon billions of patterns possible with the DNA polymer—or "polynucleotide"—there are only a finite number and at least one of them would produce another Christ.

Thus, if Jesus was God and his divinity was dependant on his being born of a virgin, then modern genetic techniques could create another Christ through genetic manipulation techniques. I think most orthodox Christians would find this possibility unacceptable.

So if Christians wish to believe Jesus was God Incarnate, they presumably must assume his divinity was a spiritual characteristic of his soul and mind and not of his human form. But if that's the case, why the necessity for a virgin birth? If the divine nature of Christ did not depend on the way the human form was produced, what could be gained by the awkward artificial creation of a totally human fetus when it could be produced so naturally by the usual sexual union between a man and woman?

Then there are the other "nature miracles." For instance, Jesus supposedly walked on water. The problem with this is best represented by what the young son of a friend of mine asked his mother while he was taking a bath: "Mommy, did the baby Jesus walk on his bathwater? If he did, how could he take a bath?"

But on a more serious note, this whole business about walking on water is terribly impressive when you first hear about it, but as soon as you try to visualize the scene, you run into problems. The three Gospels that recount this story—Mark 6:48, Matt. 14:22, and John 6:16—claim that there was a big wind blowing because the disciples were having a difficult time making any headway in their boat. Then they say they saw Jesus walking to them on the water from the shore. Did he ride up and down on the waves caused by the big wind, or did he simply walk through them? The picture presented by the first possibility is much too ridiculous to be taken seriously with Jesus flipping up into the air on the crest of a wave and then plunging down into the trough. But if he walked *through* the waves, you can't say he was walking *on* the water but only that he was apparently walking on something solid and level as if he were on a spit of land. That should give you pause about the miraculous nature of the event.[30]

What about the feeding of the five thousand? This is one story that is included in all four of the Gospels so it is apparent that his followers were very impressed by this seemingly miraculous event. Obviously, there is nothing in modern science that could account for the spontaneous production of so much food out of five loaves and two fishes. But there is a great deal that can be explained psychologically. It's a prime directive of

---

[30] Only Matthew claims that the boat was "many furlongs" from the land, and he alone tells the story of Peter joining Jesus on the water, only to sink when he became afraid. Jesus' resulting exclamation, "Oh man of little faith, why did you doubt," sounds more like Matthew chastising contemporary skeptics who doubted that Jesus really walked on water. Few scholars take this sole addendum to the tale seriously.

humans to take along the necessities for life when they leave their homes for a trip or an outing—especially one in which there is little chance for replenishment. But even in the modern Western world with its plethora of mini-marts and fast-food restaurants, who hasn't taken a trip where the mother has insisted on packing a lunch and some snacks for everyone "just in case." It's instinctive, especially in a primitive place like the Galilean desert in the first century. The miracle here lies in the way Jesus demonstrated to his followers how they are to act with one another by sharing his and his disciples' meager supplies with everyone else and not keeping them just for themselves. Lo and behold, suddenly there is more than enough for everyone as each group starts to share their personal "just-in-case" supplies with their neighbors. And as for the baskets of food left over, if you can't figure out how that happened, you've never been to a bring-your-own, pot-luck church social and had to clean up afterwards. There's always enough food left over to re-feed the same crowd.

However, when we come to the healing miracles, we can't really be as certain that science or logic can cast doubts on them. Many scientists and doctors are willing to admit today that there are some spontaneous cures that are impossible to explain medically. The remarkably stringent conditions for accepting a miracle at Lourdes is a case in point. Many cures that are rejected by Lourdes' non-sectarian doctors would seem to ordinary laymen to be very persuasive, indeed, making the ones they do accept that much more remarkable.

So it behooves us to take a closer look at the healings of Jesus and what they may indicate.

The Healing Miracles: Perhaps the Key to Understanding Jesus

The one aspect of Jesus's ministry that most modern Biblical scholars want to avoid is the question of the healing miracles. Usually they pass them off by noting that healings were the coin of the day in the first century, that no prophet was worth his salt if he didn't perform them. That may be true but it's obvious that something a great deal more significant than the run-of-the-mill healings of the revivalist-tent variety was going on with the healing miracles that Jesus was performing. Although later generations would put perhaps more emphasis on the remarkable things Jesus said, it was what he did that attracted the large crowds during his ministry. He complained about the way people wanted him to give them a sign that he was someone special. But then he almost always obliged them by curing someone who was disabled. Consider Mark 2:3-12:

> And they came, bringing to him a paralytic carried by
> four men. And when they could not get near him because
> of the crowd, they removed the roof above him; and when
> they had made an opening, they let down the pallet on

which the paralytic lay. And when Jesus saw their faith, he said to the paralytic, "My son, your sins are forgiven." Now some of the scribes were sitting there, questioning in their hearts, "Why does this man speak thus? It is blasphemy! Who can forgive sins but God alone?" And immediately Jesus, perceiving in his spirit that they thus questioned within themselves, said to them, "Why do you question thus in your hearts? Which is easier, to say to the paralytic, 'Your sins are forgiven,' or to say, 'Rise, take up your pallet and walk'? But that you may know that the Son of Man has authority on earth to forgive sins" --he said to the paralytic-- "I say to you, rise, take up your pallet and go home." And he rose, and immediately took up the pallet and went out before them all; so that they were all amazed and glorified God, saying, "We never saw anything like this!"[31]

It is obvious from this account that Jesus thought people would be convinced that he had the right to declare that their sins were forgiven if he gave them a demonstration of his power to heal even the most grievous of disabilities. [32] That meant that he, himself, could have been convinced he was someone special by the same evidence of his healing ability.

Let's take a look at the basic bare-bones history of Jesus as recounted in Mark. Jesus is baptized by John, a charismatic preacher who proclaims the coming of the Kingdom of God. As soon as he's baptized, Jesus retires to the desert for a long time, probably longer than the 40 days recounted in the Gospel since that's a euphemism often used by the ancients to indicate an extended period. Mark says in 1:13, "And he was in the wilderness forty days, tempted by Satan; and he was with the wild beasts; and the angels ministered to him." Since no one was with Jesus when he had these experiences, we have to assume that either Jesus recounted them to his disciples or they were added by the author of Mark to account for the kind of things Jesus said and did after he returned from the desert. Remember, according to Mark Jesus performed no miracles and made no reference to himself as the Son of Man before his baptism and retreat to the desert. And indeed there seems to have been no preaching before either because as Mark says in 6:1-3:

> He went away from there and came to his own country; and his disciples followed him. And on the Sabbath he began to teach in the synagogue; and many who heard him were astonished, saying, "Where did this man get all

---

[31] The same story is found in Luke 5:18-26 and also in an abbreviated form in Matthew 9:2-8.

[32] An interesting question here: was Jesus actively forgiving the man's sins or was he really saying that he knew that everyone's sins were already forgiven? Those who've had a near death experience claim the latter.

this? What is the wisdom given to him? What mighty works are wrought by his hands! Is not this the carpenter, the son of Mary and brother of James and Joses and Judas and Simon, and are not his sisters here with us?" And they took offense at him.

If he had preached at the synagogue and healed people before his sojourn in the desert, his relatives and neighbors would never have reacted in this way. So it looks as if they thought Jesus was just an ordinary man who grew up in their town but who was suddenly starting to speak with an authority they weren't willing to grant him. "Just who does he think he is?" seems to be the general attitude, not the reaction one would expect had he "revealed" his messianic nature before.[33]

If we assume that all the miraculous pronouncements by God at Jesus' baptism were later additions by the Gospel authors or the scribes, then Jesus becomes just one of the many followers of John the Baptizer, looking to wash away his sins before John's predicted arrival of the Kingdom. But something drives him to seek more. Why else would he go into isolation in the desert for such a long time? If he considered himself the Messiah at this time, his decision makes no sense. But if he's looking for enlightenment, for some sort of transformation, then it makes a great deal of sense.

What if Jesus did receive a transforming experience that convinced him that he was more than just an ordinary man? He wasn't the first to have such a conviction and he certainly wouldn't be the last. What made his conviction apparently carry so much more weight was the remarkable success he had to heal the most serious of illnesses.

All of the Synoptic Gospels, but especially the earliest Gospel of Mark, speak of the large crowds and their pushing and shoving to get near him to such an extent that Mark says he was forced to get into a boat to get some breathing room so that he could speak to them. The extremes that people were willing to go to in order to experience his healing powers is typified by the above account of the friends actually removing a roof in order to lower a paralytic to him—a story so bizarre and yet so compassionately human that it achieves an unusual credibility. All of this bespeaks of a healing ability that was unique even for a time when miracle-working prophets were supposedly a dime a dozen.

So now we have an ordinary man, so deeply inspired by this Baptizer in the wilderness who was "clothed in camel's hair" and eating "locusts and wild honey" that he decided to drop everything and follow John's example by fasting and praying in the desert. What really happened

---

[33] The early childhood stories found only in Luke of the boy Jesus instructing the elders in the synagogue are considered by most scholars to be added by the author of Luke to support the contention that Jesus was messianic from birth. Paul, Mark, Matthew, and John obviously never heard of them.

to him we'll never know, but he came out a changed man, speaking with a wisdom and compassion and performing miracles that astonished everyone who met him.

But Who Did *He* think He was?

Scholars have puzzled for ages over Jesus' reference to himself as the "Son of Man." There are two conflicting opinions: (1) that he used that expression to identify himself with mankind, not as a deity but as a human being; (2) that he was implying that he was the Messiah without coming right out and saying so. No one else ever refers to him as the Son of Man even though it is recorded that Jesus did so in no fewer than 81 places in the Gospels—14 in the Gospel of Mark, 30 in Matthew, 25 in Luke, and 12 in John. There is no mention of this title in the Epistles of Paul or any of the other Epistles, nor can it be found in any of the later liturgies of the Church—the Son of God, yes; the Son of Man, no. Why? The supporters of the first view that the term means a human among humans point to Psalm 8:4-5...

> What is man, that thou art mindful of him? and the son of man, that thou visitest him? For thou hast made him a little lower than the angels...

...and also to Ezekiel 2:1 ff:

> And he said to me, "Son of man, stand upon your feet and I will speak with you."...And he said to me [again] "Son of man, I send you to the people of Israel...And you, son of man, be not afraid of them, nor be afraid of their words...

It is interesting that this phrase is repeated 87 times in reference to Ezekiel, a prophet but a very human man nonetheless. Jesus himself equates the term "the sons of men" to humanity in Mark 3:28:

> "Truly, I say to you, The sons of men will have forgiveness for all their sins and for all the evil words they say:"[34]

Why then wouldn't this indicate that he thought the term meant the same thing when he used it in reference to himself?

However, there are those who think that Jesus used the term to indicate his messianic nature because of the way in which it was used in Daniel 7:13-14:

> I saw in the night visions, and, behold, one like the *Son of man* [35] came with the clouds of heaven, and came to the

---

[34] A sentiment repeated by those who have experienced an NDE, giving even more credence to the idea that he was declaring what he knew rather than what he thought he could grant as the Messiah.

[35] The New Revised Standard version of the Bible translates this as "one like a human being."

> Ancient of days, and they brought him near before him.
> And there was given him dominion, and glory, and a
> kingdom, that all people, nations, and languages, should
> serve him: his dominion is an everlasting dominion,
> which shall not pass away, and his kingdom that which
> shall not be destroyed.

Even though the authorship of the Book of Daniel is questioned today by many scholars, it was an accepted part of Hebrew scripture at the time of Jesus. Did he expect the people around him to understand that he was referring to this passage in Daniel and that he was the Messiah that Daniel predicted? Or did Jesus' persistent use of the term actually refer to *an ambivalence in himself?*

Just what exactly was he? He knew he was a man, but apparently he was also more than a man. Certainly he was more than the men around him in wisdom as well as miraculous abilities. Wouldn't the phrase, Son of Man, with its inherent ambiguity exactly express his own conviction that he was certainly more than just any other man, but just as certainly not God? Nowhere is this ambiguity more clearly expressed than in Mark 8:27:

> And Jesus went on with his disciples, to the villages of
> Caesarea Philippi; and on the way he asked his disciples,
> "Who do men say that I am?" And they told him, "John
> the Baptist; and others say, Elijah; and others one of the
> prophets." And he asked them, "But who do you say that I
> am?" Peter answered him, "You are the Christ."[36] And he
> charged them to tell no one about him.[37]

The orthodox say that Jesus was testing his disciples to see if they had finally recognized his messianic nature. That isn't the way it reads. Here is a man who, according to Mark, was never considered an exceptional person by his family and friends, and certainly didn't perform any miracles before he was baptized by John and went into the desert. The sojourn in the desert changed him radically. All of a sudden he is exhibiting powers and wisdom far beyond anything he or his contemporaries have ever seen in a world that was expecting spectacular events to occur at any moment. Whatever role he will be playing in these coming events, he is convinced that it must be one of great significance. That's why he's calling himself the Son of Man.

But although he suspects because of the signs he's performing that maybe he really is the Messiah, he needs the corroboration of his peers. After all, only a few weeks or months ago he was no different than anyone else. Once he is convinced by Peter's declaration that he is the Messiah, he realizes that it must be he who fulfills the prophecies and brings about the apocalyptic end of the world by doing something spectacular in Jerusalem,

---

[36] Or in other translations, "the Anointed," or "the Messiah."
[37] See also Matthew 16:13 and Luke 9:18.

which was not only the center of the Jewish world but in their minds the center of the whole material universe. So he starts to prepare for his totally uncharacteristic triumphal entry into Jerusalem as a conquering king accompanied by the crowds that have come to be devoted to him throughout his ministry.[38] And this at a time when the Romans were on a hair trigger because of the significance of the Passover—the celebration by the Jews of their last great liberation from bondage. Why else did he turn over the money-changer's tables in the temple right under the noses of the Roman garrison unless he was deliberately attempting to bring about the end?

If we are to believe the scenario that I have outlined here, then the events leading up to his trip to Jerusalem take on a different aspect. Consider for example his "prediction" in Mark 11:1-7:

> And when they drew near to Jerusalem, to Bethpage and Bethany, at the Mount of Olives, he sent two of his disciples, and said to them, "Go into the village opposite you, and immediately as you enter it you will find a colt tied, on which no one has ever sat; untie it and bring it. If any one says to you, 'Why are you doing this?' say, 'The Lord has need of it and will send it back here immediately.'" And they went away, and found a colt tied at the door out in the open street; and they untied it. And those who stood there said to them, "What are you doing, untying the colt?" And they told them what Jesus had said; and they let them go. And they brought the colt to Jesus, and threw their garments on it; and he sat upon it.

No one in a country as poor as this one would ever let a stranger take away an expensive and prestigious commodity like a horse unless this had been arranged beforehand. And why would Jesus decide to ride into Jerusalem on a frisky colt like a Roman general astride a young steed and cheered by his faithful followers, unless he wanted to give the impression that he was a conquering hero? [39] Not only that, but he tops off his triumphant entry by turning over the money tables in the temple after entering the city, a totally uncharacteristic action by the Jesus described in the Synoptic Gospels.

---

[38] Some have pointed out the strange behavior of the Jerusalem citizens welcoming Jesus as a conquering hero one week and calling for his crucifixion the next, a rather unbelievable switch of allegiance. It makes more sense if we assume that his triumphal entry was accompanied by his devoted followers from the countryside, not the citizens of Jerusalem who according to Mark didn't even know him. Once the Romans entered the picture, the peasants scattered, leaving only the urban mobs who would just as soon see this country rube put in his place.

[39] Only Matt 21:2 mentions an ass when he quotes Jesus saying "you will find an ass tied, and a colt with her" in order to claim that this was to "fulfill what was spoken by the prophet," (Zech 9:9): "...Behold, your king is coming to you, humble, and mounted on an ass, and on a colt, the foal of an ass." But if you're not trying to force the actual events to fit with ancient predictions of the Messiah, then you're just left with a frisky colt. There's nothing humble about this entry.

The preparations for the Passover meal that came to be known as the Last Supper are even more revealing as told in Mark 14:13-16:

> And he sent two of his disciples, and said to them, "Go into the city, and a man carrying a jar of water will meet you; follow him, and wherever he enters, say to the householder, 'The Teacher says, Where is my guest room, where I am to eat the Passover with my disciples?' And he will show you a large upper room furnished and ready; there prepare for us." And the disciples set out and went to the city, and found it as he had told them; and they prepared the Passover.

Now instead of a miraculous prediction, this story obviously describes an arrangement that Jesus had already made without the knowledge of the disciples. In fact it sounds just like the spy stories we are so familiar with— "When you get to the train station, follow the man with the rose in his lapel and he'll lead you to the safe house where the password is 'the boss needs a room'." Pretty standard stuff.

Then there's the problem of poor old Judas. Even before the Passover, Mark 14:10 has him scurrying to the chief priests to betray Jesus to them when the opportunity is right. In the light of the elaborate preparations that Jesus has made in secret for the Passover, this starts to take on the aspect of yet another preparation made with the aid of an obscure disciple hardly mentioned in the Gospels before this seemingly traitorous moment. Nowhere is there ever any hint of the kind of discontent that would have had to be inherent in a follower to be able to commit such an act of betrayal on his own. Judas would have had to have been the loud and contentious character depicted in the musical *Jesus Christ Superstar* for him to have acted in this way. Such a previous demeanor would never have escaped the notice of the Gospel writers if it really happened, especially in light of what he eventually did.

In the entourage of charismatic leaders, there are always quiet sycophants whose devotion to their leaders is total and without question. It seems to me that Judas could easily be such a person—the faithful and unquestioning follower. Such a man would never do anything without the express approval and encouragement of his beloved master. If Schweitzer is right and Jesus really sought to die to bring about the Kingdom of God, then Judas could have been incorporated into Jesus' plans to make that sacrifice a reality. And when that plot is successful and Jesus is crucified, Judas hangs himself, not in remorse, but in the eager anticipation that he will rejoin his beloved master in paradise.

Unfortunately for this scenario to be real, we have to question the phrases that Jesus supposedly said publicly condemning the actions of Judas. He says that he knows that one of the twelve sitting at the table with him will betray him. And he concludes by saying in Mark 14:21, "…woe to that man by whom the Son of man is betrayed! It would have been better for that man if he had not been born." You wouldn't think that Jesus would say something like that if he were the one who commanded Judas to perform the betrayal.

But let's suppose for a moment that Judas did betray Jesus on his own and that Jesus really said this. Once Judas realizes that Jesus *miraculously* knows about his plot to betray him, why would he persist in his plans? He's been discovered and surely he would never persist and chance the wrath of his fellow disciples and the prediction of his doom by this apparently superhuman god-like man. Since it seems highly unlikely that he would, that would imply that these phrases were either misinterpreted or added later to avoid the implication that Jesus was preparing for his own arrest. After all, if no betrayal is involved, then the events that follow look very much like they were preplanned by Jesus, himself, just as the secret arrangements for the entry into the city and the Last Supper were preplanned. That of course would never do if we are to believe that Jesus was the Messiah. So even as early as in the oral traditions, it would have been natural for the tellers of the tale to portray the arrest as the result of a betrayal and not as a plot to bring about the final apocalypse.

And then there is the recently surfaced *Gospel of Judas*, a Coptic Egyptian translation of a 2nd Century Greek manuscript, condemned in 180 C.E. by our old friend Bishop Irenaeus. Many months after I had included the above speculations about Judas in my original manuscript, an official translation was offered to the public of this rediscovered Gospel which, much to my delight, actually confirms those speculations, albeit with a Gnostic slant that reflects the writer's prejudicial point of view.

The Gospel of Judas

Without question this gospel is a Gnostic document which supports the contention that an evil Demiurge created the physical world, and that there is an exalted super deity who is far superior to this inferior creator god. Jesus wants to shed "the man who clothes me" and return to the realm of that exalted being. He therefore instructs Judas as his most favored disciple to turn him over to the authorities so that he can assume his rightful place in the heavenly realm away from this evil material world.

This is depicted as a joyful occasion with Jesus laughing in delight that he will finally return to that heavenly realm from whence he came. In fact, one of the more delightful characteristics of this gospel is that Jesus laughs often in it in contrast to the rather solemn Jesus depicted in the Canonical Gospels.

The Gospel ends with the betrayal of Jesus portrayed as the crowning achievement of Judas. There is no crucifixion or resurrection stories here because the last thing Jesus would want to do according to this

Gnostic writer would be to return to this evil material world after achieving the Gnostic's goal of separation from it.

Consider the Stark Contrast to the Jesus in Mark

However, in Mark 14:32ff Jesus prays to God in fearful uncertainty about the coming events that he has set in motion:

> And they went to a place which was called Gethsemane; and he said to his disciples, "Sit here, while I pray." And he took with him Peter and James and John, and began to be greatly distressed and troubled. And he said to them, "My soul is very sorrowful, even to death; remain here, and watch." And going a little farther, he fell on the ground and prayed that, if it were possible, the hour might pass from him. And he said, "Abba, Father,[40] all things are possible to thee; remove this cup from me..."

Three times he falls to the ground and begs God to let him off the hook. Does this really sound like a self-confident Messiah talking, fully aware that he and God are one and the same? For instance, although Matthew and Luke repeat this tale of Jesus' vacillation, John eliminates it completely since its all-too-human emotion doesn't fit in with his theme of Jesus as the resolute Son of God fearlessly striding towards his fate to redeem mankind.

In addition, Jesus tells Peter, James, and John to stay and "watch." Watch for what? Could it be the arrival of the Kingdom that Jesus may very well have been asking God to initiate? After all, the disciples really didn't know what he was praying for since he had deliberately gone a little way away from them so that they supposedly wouldn't have been able to hear him. And why did he bring them with him in the first place unless it was to join him when the Kingdom came?

So Who Is the Man Behind the Gospel Wall?

According to the opinion expressed here, and that of a growing number of biblical scholars, Jesus was not God Incarnate. Nor do we believe that the original Jewish Christians[41] or the author of the Gospel of Thomas thought he was anything other than the human Messiah. After all, the Messiah of Jewish tradition was not considered to be God. That would have been anathema to the Hebraic tradition that there was only one God. Worship of any other entity, whether it be human, animal, or idol, was blasphemy. The punishment was death by stoning, a fate that the first martyr Stephen experienced and the apostle Paul barely escaped.

---

[40] Again, we have to wonder with the Arians, do the orthodox really think Jesus was talking to himself here?

[41] Such as the Ebionites who maintained that Christians must follow all of the Jewish laws including the dietary laws and circumcision. They did not believe that Jesus was God.

Godhood was bestowed upon Jesus by many early Christians including the author of the Gospel of John, the apostle Paul, and Bishop Irenaeus who condemned as heretics all those who didn't believe that Jesus was the unique Son of God. However, it's no wonder that the majority of the orthodox Jews could never accept this doctrine of God splitting himself into two entities, let alone three.

But I said at the beginning of this chapter that I thought Jesus was a great deal more than *just* the Son of God. That sounds like an oxymoron—how could anyone be more than God Incarnate? Well consider this: If Jesus was not only a man but also the creator of this vast universe, then what's so wonderful about his performing a few miracles? That's like praising Pavarotti for being able to sing "Jingle Bells." But if he was as human as you or I, then his healing powers and his wisdom should be the subjects of awe and wonder. It opens the door to a human ability and a human destiny that few would have considered possible.

We will discuss these later but before we move on to them, let's consider the questions about Jesus raised in this chapter.

Did Jesus really expect the end of the world to occur at his death, and more to the point, did he think he could bring it about? I find the arguments of Schweitzer on this score to be compelling, and the more I consider the *immediacy statements*, the more I am convinced that Jesus really said them and really believed that some of the people listening to him would experience the "end of time." His uncharacteristic acts of riding into Jerusalem as a conquering king and his trashing of the temple lends great credence to the idea that he really thought any attempt by the powers of the physical world to kill him would initiate the events that would bring in the Kingdom of God. That argument becomes even more compelling when you consider that the author of John's Gospel changed the timing of the trashing of the temple to the beginning of his ministry to avoid the obvious implication that Jesus was deliberately provoking the authorities to attack him. If the author of the last written Gospel thought that, many of his contemporaries must have thought the same thing. But when the apocalypse didn't happen in the followers' lifetimes, the author of John had to change the sequence to maintain Jesus' credibility as the sacrificial Lamb of God.

And then we must consider Jesus' persistent use of the expression, "Son of Man." Those who are convinced he was the Messiah say he was referring to the passages we've mentioned in Daniel to hide from his enemies the fact that he thought of himself as the Messiah while allowing his followers to believe that he was. Others are equally convinced that he was trying to show that he thought of himself as a man—an exceptional man to be sure, but still just a man. However, Jesus may very well have used the term because he wasn't sure exactly *what* he was or what his role was in the coming messianic events that were on everyone's mind.

I think it was only after the continuing exhibition of his extraordinary healing powers and the unquestioning adulation of his closest companions that he finally came to the conclusion that he must be the expected Messiah. Once he made that assumption, it became obvious that it was up to him to bring about the expected apocalypse and the establishment of God's Kingdom on earth.

The fact that Jesus was mistaken identifies him as a fallible human who was at the same time an extraordinary man capable of extraordinary things. The interesting thing about this is that if he had not made this fundamental mistake, we probably wouldn't know anything about him. The story of the crucifixion and resurrection is a powerful and compelling one that has lasted undiminished for 2000 years. Without it Jesus would have no doubt faded into the background of the other aspiring messiahs of the first century. With it we have the opportunity of examining the life of a truly unique individual who managed to realize his transcendent nature, a divine nature that I am convinced is present in all of us.

But if Jesus' transformation was only manifested after his sojourn in the desert, then one has to wonder if other humans could also be transformed.

Jesus' Desert Experience

The question is, what transformed Jesus into the remarkable man he became while he presumably meditated in the desert after his baptism by John? Some have said that maybe both he and John contacted the Essene community at Qumran since there are some similarities between the Dead Sea Scrolls and the messages that both John and Jesus preached. That may be true for John the Baptizer, but it is doubtful that Jesus received his stunning transformation while he was with the Essenes. There is nothing written in the scrolls about Jesus. If the Essenes had witnessed the amazing transformation of Jesus, they would have no doubt assumed he was the "Teacher of Light" that the scrolls claimed was coming to lead them in their fight with the forces of darkness.

On the other hand, the messages people have received in near-death experiences [42] are remarkably similar to the ones Jesus preached during his ministry—love your neighbor as yourself; do unto others what you would have them do unto you; loving God and loving your fellow man are the two most important commandments; don't worry so much about what to eat or wear, but "consider the lilies of the field that toil not, neither do they spin, yet Solomon in all his glory was not arrayed like one of these."

All of this, of course, is simply speculation. But if you accept that after he had some kind of experience in his solitude in the desert, Jesus changed from an ordinary carpenter or laborer into an amazing miracle healer and inspired teacher, then it isn't unreasonable to assume that an event that led to similar, albeit less profound, experiences by many ordinary

---

[42] See Chapter 6 for a full discussion of the near-death experience.

people could have been the cause of Jesus' stunning transformation. And looking at it in another way, while it may have been necessary for his followers to make him into Christ to give his message the authority of God, Himself, we now have the experiences of thousands of people which corroborate his message, and there is no longer any need to turn him into God Almighty.

But in the very act of turning Jesus into God, early Christians inadvertently revealed a truth about their own spiritual condition. Once Jesus becomes strictly human, his elevation by his devoted followers into a being that is more than what we seemingly are has lifted all of us to new realms of possibilities.

Nowhere is this more clearly shown than in the speculations about the nature of the Trinity by a third Century theological genius, Origen of Alexandria (185-252 C.E.). He speculated that all souls must have been created by God before there was a physical world—in essence, he was suggesting that we are all transcendent and eternal. However, these souls of ours were unable to accomplish the purpose for which they were made, namely the eternal contemplation of God, and were therefore incorporated into the physical world as humans in order to learn how to achieve that goal. Origen postulated that Jesus was the one exception who contemplated God so successfully that he became almost indistinguishable from Him just as a red hot bar of iron becomes indistinguishable from the fire which heats it. Thus, it was possible for Jesus to become both human and divine.

That's what can happen to us, or at least that's what Origen is really saying because the first half of his story is an attempt to make Jesus uniquely divine in a way that's different from the rest of us. Once that misconception is put to rest, his idea of Christianity becomes a paean to the human soul. If Christ is in Jesus, then Christ must be in us.

Nowhere is this more clearly expressed than in the Omega theory of Jesus by Teilhard de Chardin, a French Jesuit priest, who from a completely different point of view comes to the same conclusion about the direction humanity could be taking to fulfill its destiny.

Chapter 5

Teilhard de Chardin and Humanity's Destiny

Just as life evolved from the protozoa, all of existence seems to have evolved as well. Nowhere is this more explicitly developed than by a French Jesuit paleontologist, Teilhard de Chardin, who traced the evolution of matter from the original energy soup of the Big Bang to the mega-molecules of life. According to Teilhard, not only just matter, but the spiritual world itself is evolving to an ultimate goal that represents the destiny of all mankind.

Teilhard de Chardin and the Piltdown Man

Pierre Teilhard de Chardin (1881-1955) put forward in his book, *The Phenomenon of Man*, the proposition that Jesus represented the ultimate Omega of mankind's spiritual destiny. As both a paleontologist and Jesuit, Teilhard attempted to marry science and his Jesuit-based religion, and in doing so managed to alienate not only the scientific community but his own ecclesiastical bosses as well. As a result he was forbidden to teach his theories and was forced to withhold his work from publication during his lifetime. Friends later published the hidden manuscript after his death.

His cause was not advanced among scientists or philosophers when in 1953 the famous Piltdown Man which he supposedly helped discover and identify as genuine was revealed to be a deliberate fraud. In 1912 a human skull and an apelike jaw which seemed to fit perfectly together were found at the Piltdown quarry in Sussex, England, and claimed by amateur archaeologist Charles Dawson and the prominent Arthur Smith Woodward, keeper of paleontology at the British Museum, to be the "missing link" between ape and man. Teilhard, as a young assistant, later discovered a tooth at the site that helped to confirm that conclusion. Although there were some skeptics, Piltdown was generally hailed as a major find of great significance since it fit in nicely with the then current ideas of mankind's evolution. Teilhard's reputation as a promising young paleontologist was established by this seemingly monumental discovery. But when it was discovered that the Piltdown skull and jawbone had been artificially altered to make them fit together, that reputation was put into severe jeopardy.

Serious Paleontologist or Pious Fraud?

Currently, Dawson, who died in 1917, is thought to be the sole perpetrator, but in 1980 Stephen Jay Gould put forward his idea that

Teilhard was a co-conspirator. No one but Gould holds this questionable theory but he has an axe to grind—he hates with a vengeance Teilhard's analysis of evolution and wants to taint it by destroying the reputation of its author. However, others have pointed out that although Teilhard could no doubt be capable of perpetuating a hoax as a spur-of-the-moment student's joke, Piltdown required extensive preparation over years and an expertise unlikely to be found in such an inexperienced young man. In addition, the skull and jawbone had been "seeded" at the site and actually discovered by workmen digging there—no one else was present. In any case it was not too surprising that he should follow the lead of his mentor in authenticating the find when in fact many much-more experienced paleontologists, like, Marcellin Boule, a greatly respected anthropologist, and the aforementioned Arthur Smith Woodward were guilty of the same mistake. After all, it *did* imply that the origin of mankind resided in the British Isles, and that fit in perfectly with the 1912 notion that England was the most civilized nation on the planet. Pride of Empire, don't you know.

As we said, no one but Gould points to Teilhard as a perpetrator. Indeed, much more attention has been directed at a plethora of others who have been under suspicion, including Sir Arthur Conan Doyle, paleontologist Martin Hinton, geologist W. J. Sollas, and many others connected with the discovery including Hargreaves, Abbot, Barlow, and Butterfield. But when it was discovered that all of the many previous discoveries by Dawson were also forgeries, there was little question that he and he alone was guilty..

When push comes to shove, it's no more sensible to paint Teilhard's theories as the questionable works of a pious fraud than it is to claim that a love for vegetables, children, and classical music makes Adolph Hitler a sensitive humanitarian.[1] The only criteria that should be applied here is the legitimacy of his concepts as they stand on their own.

Teilhard de Chardin's Theory

Teilhard says that "matter has obeyed from the beginning that great law of biology to which we shall have to recur time and time again, the law of 'complexification.'" [2] This is the theme that runs through all of Teilhard's treatise, that everything, from matter to life, has become more complex over the immense expanse of time from the Big Bang 13.7 billion years ago to the present. Matter itself didn't even exist at the very beginning but was simply energy before it cooled enough to form the simplest atoms of hydrogen and helium. Since then it has taken the operation of novas and supernovas to create the more complex elements and eventually the

---

[1] Or that President Clinton's immoral acts made him a bad president. As one elderly lady said when asked what she thought of Clinton, "Oh, I think the scum bag's doing a pretty good job!"

[2] Teilhard de Chardin, *The Phenomenon of Man*, Harper Torchbooks, Harper & Row, New York, translated from the French by Bernard Wall, 1959, p. 48.

molecules that constitute the material world we see about us today. "The stars are laboratories in which the evolution of matter proceeds in the direction of large molecules..."[3]

But what about the theory of entropy, that law that says all energy must eventually diminish to its lowest level, that everything must become more random as time progresses? Although he doesn't speak in the following quote about entropy as such, he implies it when he says:

> ...the evolution of matter reveals itself to us...as a process during which the constituents of the atom are inter-combined and ultra-condensed. Qualitatively, this transformation now appears to us as a definite, but costly, operation in which an original impetus slowly becomes exhausted. Laboriously, step by step, the atomic and molecular structures become higher and more complex, but the upward force is lost on the way. Moreover, the same wearing away that is gradually consuming the cosmos in its totality is at work within the terms of the synthesis, and the higher the terms the quicker this action takes place. Little by little, the *improbable* combinations that they represent become broken down again into more simple components, which fall back and are disaggregated in the shapelessness of *probable* distributions.[4]

Thus it appears that complexification is a prime characteristic of the evolving universe even though eventually entropy will have its way and reduce everything to its ultimate random distribution.

The Complexification of Life

Teilhard observes that science has always been concerned with the externality of things while religion has concentrated on the internal, which is the major reason they are always at odds with one another. But when we come to the material thing called "humanity," science dismisses consciousness as an inappropriate subject for consideration, as an anomaly. He claims that by restricting thought and consciousness to the human, science uses that "as an excuse for eliminating it from its models of the universe." This makes no more sense than it would have been to eliminate radium as an abnormal substance because radiation had never been detected in other material substances. In fact, it is impossible to evade the *within-ness* of man because it is "the substance of all knowledge."

For Teilhard this "rent" in the fabric of the universe allows us to see an internal characteristic that must be evident in all material substance because of the underlying unity of all things. Everything in the universe

---

[3] *Ibid*, p. 50.
[4] *Ibid*, p. 52.

came from the Big Bang—therefore, everything must be connected, must be part of the same *stuff*. If there is a *within-ness* of things at just one point, namely mankind, then it must extend throughout all of creation.

Life, then, must be inherent in the very subatomic particles that make up the atoms and molecules that eventually result in the giant protein molecules of living things. Therefore, to put our ideas about transcendence in Teilhard's terminology, free will indicates a *within-ness* of humanity that is not totally controlled by the deterministic nature of material substance. But if Teilhard is correct that this *within-ness* cannot be accepted as an anomaly that exists only in humans, then our less complex relatives in the brotherhood of life must also exhibit some self-determination, some primitive free will. And as we go down the food chain, that self-determination gets less and less until we come to inanimate matter, a reverse example of what Teilhard means by "the complexification of life."

But how do we get to this complexification in the first place? Through something which Teilhard calls *convergence*. In the beginning there was only energy which eventually converged into the simplest of atoms, hydrogen, which consists of only one proton and one electron. As time progressed, more complex atoms like helium with two protons, two neutrons, and two electrons converged out of the cooling primeval soup which in turn combined in their trillions upon trillions to form stars. Super novas produced heavier and heavier elements on up the Periodic Table until the material universe as we know it emerged. Atoms converged to form molecules of more and more complexity until we come to the mega-molecules of cellular life.

Whatever one might think of Teilhard's idea of the presence of some kind of transcendence in all material substance, there can be no argument about this progression of complexity in the material universe. The universe started with zero complexity at the start of the Big Bang and progressed through billions of years of complexification to result in the maximum complexity of the present. If we care to observe it, we see all around us the decay of energy from a high potential to a lower one, from order to chaos, from creation to decay. Things run down just as the theory of entropy says they will—except when we examine the act of creation, itself, and realize that its initial thrust created all of life's complexity.

The engine for all of this convergence actually came from the initial Big Bang, itself, which was passed on to the individual energy sources in the billions of created stars. The entropy of the entire closed system of the universe is indeed increasing because its total energy is diminishing just as the law predicts. But individual stars within the universe are pumping energy into their planetary systems, decreasing their entropy and generating the complexification that can result in intelligent life. Eventually, even this reversal of entropy will be defeated when the energy of each star runs out and they die along with their surrounding planets. *But what will emerge before that happens?*

The Progressive Spheres of Creation

Before he gets to the ultimate destiny of mankind, Teilhard describes how the various spheres of the physical world converge into the sphere of life—the biosphere—which includes all life forms from the simplest to the most complex. As he says:

> Geologists have for long agreed in admitting the zonal composition of our planet. We have already spoken of the barysphere, central and metallic, surrounded by the rocky lithosphere that in turn is surrounded by the fluid layers of the hydrosphere and the atmosphere. Since Suess, science has rightly become accustomed to add another to these four concentric layers, the living membrane composed of the fauna and flora of the globe, the *biosphere*...[5]

Once mankind appears in the picture, Teilhard claims that a new layer emerges which is unique in its own right and must be given a new name—the *noosphere*. This is the layer created by the appearance of mankind and its ability to reflect on the very process of thinking, itself. We are self-reflecting beings, and as we communicate to other self-reflecting beings, we form a new convergence increasing the complexification of society into a new entity whose nervous system is the very lines of communication we have created. As Jennifer Cobb Kreisberg put it in her 1995 article in *Wired* magazine:

> Teilhard imagined a stage of evolution characterized by a complex membrane of information enveloping the globe and fueled by human consciousness. It sounds a little off-the-wall, until you think about the Net, that vast electronic web encircling the Earth, running point to point through a nerve-like constellation of wires. We live in an intertwined world of telephone lines, wireless satellite-based transmissions, and dedicated computer circuits that allow us to travel electronically from Des Moines to Delhi in the blink of an eye.[6]

This has led to the *Gaia* hypothesis by James Lovelock and Lynn Margulis of the global ecosystem as a super-consciousness—in fact a super-organism—with all of Earth emerging as a new type of being. John Perry Barlow has called this "the creation of a collective organism of mind." For Teilhard this is the Omega condition of the world—the reason for the very existence of the universe.

---

[5] *Ibid,* p. 182.
[6] Kreisberg, Jennifer Cobb; "A Globe, Clothing Itself with a Brain," *Wired* magazine, Issue 3.06, June, 1995.

Now we come to Teilhard's synthesis of his Jesuit belief in the divinity of Jesus and the evolutionary nature of the universe he so painstakingly portrayed throughout his book. In his summary in the final chapter before his Epilogue he says,

> To make room for thought in the world, I have needed to 'interiorise' matter: to imagine an energetics of the mind; to conceive a noogenesis rising upstream against the flow of entropy; to provide evolution with a direction, a line of advance and critical points; and finally to make all things double back upon *someone.*[7]

And of course that *someone* for Teilhard is Jesus Christ, as he states in his Epilogue. He feels that without Christ we would be unaware of the Omega condition except through this examination of convergence that he has taken so much care to describe. But if Omega is already emerging, then some trace of it should be manifested in humanity, and this manifestation must be Christ. For him, Christianity is "one of the most vigorous and fruitful currents the noosphere has ever known," and "its enduring influence [is] apparent in every corner of the earth today."

It is obvious that Teilhard came to this project with an *a priori* belief in Jesus as the Son of God. But in fact, if all things "double back upon" Jesus, then Jesus must be as much the product of convergence as the Omega state is from the noosphere. Jesus doesn't have to be God incarnate in order for him to reach the culmination of the Omega state. Teilhard's superiors in the Church realized this even though he probably was somewhat ambivalent about it, himself. But it is unclear whether he was quite aware of the natural consequences of his theory as to Jesus' supposed godhood. For us it makes no difference. Most of us don't have ecclesiastical bosses that we have to placate in order to express our ideas, nor professional priestly commitments that these ideas would call into question.

It's enough for us to realize that Jesus can indeed represent the culmination of the noosphere as described by Teilhard, but perhaps not as *Omega*, the final letter of the Greek alphabet, but as *Beta,* the second letter which simply represents the next state after our current *Alpha* state. By taking away the necessity of considering Jesus as God, Himself, we don't come to the end of the process, but just the next stage, or as Teilhard would have described it, the next sphere. We don't know what ultimately will happen when we contact that transcendence experienced by Jesus and those who were apparently near death. We just assume that it will change our fundamental character, that we will become a new species, as different from our current form as *Homo sapiens sapiens* was from *Homo sapiens*, and will reveal to us the hidden transcendent nature of all reality.

---

[7] Teilhard, p. 290.

The Problem with Omega's Inevitability on Earth

As a priest, Teilhard's problem was that he was used to thinking about God in absolutist terms. Obviously, if God were infinitely good and had created the universe for the purpose of evolving humanity to its Omega destiny, the process must be inevitable. All of evolution, with its fits and starts, successes and failures, was inevitably pointed in this one direction and was preordained to be successful.

Unfortunately, that's not the way our earthly evolution works. It's Monday-morning quarterbacking to look back at Earth's past and say that since we are the result of millennia of evolution, it must have been inevitable that the progression of evolution would result in us. There is nothing in the theory of evolution that indicates that it was inevitable that an asteroid of just the right size, mass, and velocity would hit the Earth at the end of the Cretaceous Period to eliminate the dead-end dinosaurs but save the tiny mammals. After all, the earlier mass extinctions which occurred hundreds of millions of years before in the Precambrian, Cambrian, Ordovician, etc., periods resulted only in different kinds of dinosaurs, not in intelligent life.

When dealing with a single planet like Earth, the evolution of intelligent life is not inevitable. But when one considers the possibility of some sort of intelligent life evolving somewhere within this unimaginably vast universe sometime within the billions of years of its existence, the odds become considerably higher. We happen to exist on a planet where the dice came up seven. On every other planet in this solar system the dice came up snake eyes. That's undoubtedly the most common result for most solar systems in most galaxies within most super clusters. For decades the Search for Extra-Terrestrial Intelligence (SETI) has come up empty. That doesn't mean that intelligence isn't out there somewhere or wasn't out there sometime, but it does imply that it is extremely rare.

But what happens when intelligent life *does* evolve on a planet like Earth? Once we are on a closed and relatively small system—the two-dimensional curved surface of a sphere—Teilhard's ideas of the noosphere and convergence begin to be credible. However, these concepts do require the achievement of a critical point in time when connectedness is almost universal—when the global village becomes a reality. That time is now. This generation has seen an acceleration in the development of knowledge, communication, and information storage that is unprecedented in human history. It's almost as if we were on an exponential curve of ever increasing rapid development in connectedness getting closer and closer to some mathematical limit, some asymptote, in the future. As an article in a recent Discover magazine stated:

> In the 1990s some library scientists concluded that our total stockpile of information doubles every seven or eight years. A recent study at the University of California at

> Berkeley found that between 2000 and 2002, the total information in the world doubled [*in just two years*]. In many fields, such as the sciences and space technology, knowledge is accumulating at speeds that are impossible to keep up with.[8]

The question is what happens when we get very near to that limit? Do we eliminate ourselves in some cataclysm of stupidity, generating a man-made nuclear winter or an uncontrollable plague that wipes out all life on Earth? Or do we reach some sort of global spiritual enlightenment?

Decision time is rapidly approaching, and there's no guarantee that the outcome will be positive. The universe is large enough and old enough so that intelligence had a good chance of developing somewhere, sometime. But it's also big enough to handle failure. That means if earthlings eliminate themselves, the event would be a tragic dead end for us but not for the universe. The question is, what can we do to avoid becoming that dead end?

I think we as a species must focus our attention on this next stage of our development, and it is a spiritual one, not just a physical one. Life is finally in control of its own evolution, for better or worse. Physically, through DNA we will be able to reproduce ourselves in the near future, and eventually we will be able to enhance certain of our characteristics—not only our physical condition, but our mental abilities as well. Unfortunately, no laws will be able to stop this tinkering with the human condition. Mankind's curiosity is too intense to allow a tool as powerful as DNA to lie dormant.

Without the guidance of the transcendent part of our being, we are quite capable of creating monsters that will eventually cause the elimination of our humanity—if not physically then certainly spiritually. Everything that we have held dear over the millennia is in jeopardy if we don't heed the spiritual side of our natures that created our great religions, our institutions of compassion, our great works of art. When Christians created Christ out of Jesus, they put the stamp of authenticity on the things he said and did by making them the creator's explicit instructions for us. Unfortunately, we are still quite capable of genocide, global wars, and generally abominable behavior to our fellow beings despite these explicit instructions supposedly from God. What we need is the type of transformation experienced by Jesus of Nazareth. But if Jesus was human and still exhibited a spirituality that changed the world, then what can we say about this transcendent world he apparently experienced?

---

[8] *Discover*, August, 2003, p. 33.

Chapter 6

The Spiritual Search for Truth

We've already examined Christianity in detail, but let's consider all five of the major contemporary religions in a more general way. You could say that with the exception of Hinduism, which is really a kind of melting pot of many religions, each of our modern religions is based on what the statisticians would call a "sample of one." Only one or two people are considered their prime originator and their spiritual source—Abraham and Moses for Judaism, Jesus and Paul for Christianity, Muhammad for Islam, and the Buddha for Buddhism. As a data sample, that's not terribly impressive, and in fact, none of these four totally agree with one another.

It has been said that the Eastern religions lead to personal fulfillment but social stagnation while Western religions lead to social advancement but personal stagnation. That's as misleading as any generalization but it reflects a certain amount of truth. Eastern religions focus on the development of the inner soul so that it might eventually merge with the greater, external soul. Western Judaism, Christianity, and Islam concentrate on the actions of individuals as they respond to God's external commandments. Eastern spiritual development goes from the inner to the outer—Western goes from the outer to the inner.

A case can be made that without Christianity Western civilization as we now know it would have been impossible. But it's interesting that in the 60's and 70's when New Age people wanted spiritual fulfillment, they turned to the East. Part of the reason of course was because of its exotic nature, its differentness. But when they considered Christianity, many were inhibited by Christ's godly otherness and perfection that seemed to provide little chance for a mere sinful human to acquire anything close to that same transcendence. In contrast the East offered the spiritual growth that could be achieved through yoga, Zen Buddhism, and meditation techniques like Transcendental Meditation.

Of course there was the example of the Christian mystics who apparently experienced a profound transformation. But it comes at a price that few moderns are willing to pay—groveling at the feet of the utterly transcendent and concentration on minute "sins" seems much too precious to a modern mind unwilling to accept the questionable premise that all of humanity is basically sinful and can only be redeemed through Jesus Christ. The protestations of a 17th century St. Theresa of Avila on her unworthiness strike a note of hypocrisy to us in light of the self-promotional nature of those same protestations. Yet one can hardly blame Theresa and the other mystics for this ostentatious self denigration. The divine nature of the Christ seems to demand our claims of unworthiness when we attempt to approach the utter transcendence of him and our other Christian deities. How else could we fatally flawed humans come into their presence or even consider attempting to grow spiritually through our own efforts when confronted with the remote awfulness of a perfect God, Christ, Virgin Mary, or Holy Spirit?

But did those who took up the practices associated with the East grow spiritually? It's almost impossible to tell. Many seemed to acquire a new concern for their fellow humans during the social unrest of the 60's and 70's, but that included many non-religious people and traditional Christians as well. And after the turmoil of the Vietnam and Civil Rights movements passed, there was little evidence of the kind of change one would expect from a great leap forward in the evolution of the human spirit. Business as usual returned to business as usual, politicians became even more self-serving if that's possible, and the passionate young reformers became respectable middle-aged citizens. The Big Chill had definitely settled in, and the Bush Triumvirate started a disastrous and bloody war.

Should we even look for some sort of change in humanity, some evolution into a new type of being through the nurture of our spiritual nature? We have said that free will can only be possible if our minds are different from the material world. When we direct our brains to think, we must be doing it from a dimension which transcends this space-time continuum. But if this supposition is real, there should be some evidence that shows that these minds of ours can acquire information from some place other than our physical bodies. If they are truly transcendent, shouldn't there be some evidence that our minds can sense more than just the immediate present in both time and space?

The CIA's Remote Viewing (RV) Project

In 1996 a report written in the 1977 Winter issue of the CIA's classified internal publication, *Studies in Intelligence*, was made available to the public. It was called, "Parapsychology in Intelligence: A Personal Review and Conclusions," by Dr. Kenneth A. Kress, a CIA engineer with the agency's Office of Technical Services, and revealed the use of some supposedly psychic spies to view secret Soviet sites with just their minds.

In point of fact what they did was to fund a program initiated by physicists Russell Targ and Harold E. Puthoff that produced some successful results in RV at Stanford Research Institute. Ingo Swann, a self-taught psychic who had participated in a number of tests for the American Society for Psychical Research, successfully conducted a remote viewing of a site 2000 miles away selected by a skeptical CIA agent. This eventually led to the establishment of the CIA program but not without a great deal of skepticism by many in the agency. As Dr. Kress put it,

> Parapsychological data, almost by definition, are elusive and unexplained. Add a history replete with proven frauds and many people instantly reject the subject, saying, in effect, "I would not believe this stuff even if it were true." Others, who must have had personal "conversion" experiences, tend to be equally convinced that one unexplained success establishes a phenomenon. These prejudices make it difficult to evaluate parapsychology carefully and scientifically. [1]

This one paragraph neatly sums up the problem facing us with this subject. No other type of discussion leads to such black and white opinions as ones involving psychic phenomena. Yet if we want to extract any useful information about the subject, we must take a neutral position or nothing will be gained.

The advancement of knowledge depends in many cases on what the theatrical community calls a "suspension of disbelief." The Copernican concept of the heliocentric universe is a case in point. In order to accept it, one had to suspend one's astonishment that we could be on a sphere that was spinning—not an easy thing to do when all our senses were telling us that we were not. On the other hand, we shouldn't keep our minds so open that our brains fall out. And therein lies the problem. As Kress said, many intelligent practical people are unwilling to take seriously a subject like ESP which has had so much fraud, self-deception, and silliness attached to it. However, although blind belief is certainly uncalled-for, so is blind disbelief. Approaching the subject with a healthy skepticism could be productive as long as it is accompanied with a willingness to accept without prejudice the possibility that the phenomena might be real.

Remote Viewing is a technique of an extra-sensory perception or ESP that purportedly allows one to view people and sites at a distance without the use of any physical information other than the geographical coordinates of the site. If agents could be trained to use this faculty, they would be able to circumvent the Soviet's security measures and obtain classified information. As one might expect, the results were mixed.

As far as what the overall data indicated, although Kress thought that there was some validity to the effectiveness of the technique, he was unsure if he was completely unbiased:

> As a check on myself, I asked for a critique of the investigation from a disinterested consultant, a theoretical physicist with broad intellectual background. His first task was to evaluate the field of parapsychology without knowledge of the CIA data. After he had completed this critique, I asked him to acquaint himself with the CIA data and then to reassess the field. The first investigation

---

[1] Kress, Kenneth A., "Parapsychology in Intelligence: A Personal Review and Conclusions," *Studies in Intelligence*; http://www.parascope.com/ds/articles/parapsychologyDoc.htm.

produced genuine interest in paranormal functioning as a valid research area. After being acquainted with CIA data, his conclusion was, "a large body of reliable experimental evidence points to the inescapable conclusion that extrasensory perception does exist as a real phenomenon, albeit characterized by rarity and lack of reliability." This judgment by a competent scientist gave impetus to continue serious inquiry into parapsychology.[2]

In his final assessment, Kress says that, "There is no fundamental understanding of the mechanisms of paranormal functioning, and the reproducibility remains poor. The research and experiments have successfully demonstrated abilities but have not explained them nor made them reproducible."

One of the best viewers that were trained in RV was Pat Price, even though Kress admits that most of his viewings were wrong! However, enough of them were remarkably detailed direct hits that his handlers were quite optimistic. As reported in Ron Elliston's "Parapsychology in Intelligence: The Rise and Fall of the CIA's Psychic Spies":

> In late 1975, Price's CIA handlers asked him to envision several sites in Libya using RV. Price spotted clandestine training centers for guerrilla fighters and underwater demolition teams. His findings were confirmed by reconnaissance photos, and the CIA's RV unit was hopeful that the program would survive based on the success of the Libya operation. But just when things were looking up, the RV intelligence collection program was dealt a fatal blow: Price suffered a heart attack and died, and the program was effectively shut down.[3]

Due to the application orientation of the funding agencies, they had no interest in the theoretical possibilities of the technique. According to Kress, this was the reason the project was deemed unusable and caused the CIA to stop all funding. In actual fact, a number of higher ups killed the project because it conflicted with their ultra-conservative views.

But the reputation of the RV project had spread and the Defense Intelligence Agency (DIA) picked up the project and eventually renamed it Star Gate. It is this name that crops up most often these days because of the remarkable success viewers had in a number of cases, including finding a Soviet airplane which crashed in a remote jungle, the production of accurate intelligence reports during the Cuban missile crisis, and the foretelling of an Iraqi plane attack on the U.S.S. Stark in 1987. This last event was remotely

---

[2] *Ibid.*
[3] Elliston, Ron, "Parapsychology in Intelligence: The Rise and Fall of the CIA's Psychic Spies," http://www.parascope.com/ds/articles/.

viewed by Army Intelligence Officer Paul H. Smith, who has proof that he did it fifty hours before the attack took place! [4]

Dr. Jessica Utts, a Professor of Statistics at the University of California/Davis strongly asserts her belief that the tests she examined have proven remote viewing to be a real, measurable phenomenon. However, she contends that psychic ability is inborn and that it would be impossible to train agents to use it who were not born with the innate capability.

Surprisingly, none of these psychic investigators ever mentioned a commercial program which has been in existence since 1966 and which has demonstrated repeatedly an ability to train anyone—not just the psychically gifted—to view sick people at a distance and describe their illnesses.

The Remarkable Results of Silva Mind Control

Now called the Silva Method to avoid association with brain-washing techniques, this program was developed by Jose Silva, a Mexican-American from Laredo, Texas, and a self-taught electronics specialist. Knowing that one way to increase his children's chances for success as Mexican-Americans was to make them more proficient at learning, he tried using hypnosis on them to see if he could improve their IQ's or at least their ability to absorb information. To his astonishment some of them started to exhibit psychic abilities—for one thing, they were answering questions before he could ask them, including questions in Jose's mind which had nothing to do with the subject being studied. During the next 20 years from the 1940's to the 1960's he discovered that when anyone, not just his own children, was in a meditative or light-hypnotic state they were able to exhibit many ESP abilities including clairvoyance, the psychic phenomenon that gives people the ability to see things at a distance. Generally, distance viewing was most successful when the target subject being viewed was a human who was ill or under stress, even though the viewer or fledgling psychic didn't know the subject but only his or her name, age, and location.

The program that Jose eventually put together is, as one critic noted, a "hodge-podge" of seemingly unrelated techniques such as controlling headaches and pain, remembering grocery lists, using a mental alarm clock, sleeping without drugs, remembering dreams, controlling habits, losing weight, and so on. The point is that each of these techniques is taught to the students while they are meditating or in a light-hypnotic state using a great deal of mental visualization and imagination, talents that they need for the RV or "case-working" portion of the program. Thus, they are all designed to increase the students' confidence and ability to program their own minds in a way that they never experienced before while training them to use their imaginations to "see" things mentally. Only after all these

---

[4] Smith, Paul H.\; *Reading the Enemy's Mind: Inside Star Gate—America's Psychic Espionage Program*,; A Tom Doherty Associates Book; New York; 2005; pp 302-307.

techniques are learned do the students begin their clairvoyant or RV training.

At the beginning of the Silva course, the students are taught how to meditate or perform self-hypnosis to reach a state not dissimilar to the type of meditation achieved through the methods used by Eastern meditation or biological feedback. Silva calls this the *alpha* state since meditators produce strong alpha brain waves of about ten cycles per second when they're in it. Apparently, when we're wide awake, we produce brainwaves in the 15 to 40 cycles/sec range that are called beta waves. When we relax, meditate, or dream-sleep, we slip into the slower, higher-amplitude waves of alpha. Silva discovered that this was the ideal state for using the subtle "extra" senses we seem to possess.

The difference between Silva and many of the other methods of meditation is that for the Silva students this is a state they could use to perform tasks while remaining in this twilight zone of partial hypnosis — they don't just relax there passively. Students didn't "pop out" of alpha into a wide-awake beta state when they actively directed their thoughts.

Once in this alpha state, students are taught to program their minds—in effect give themselves self-hypnotic suggestions—to achieve some of the simple goals already mentioned like waking in the morning at a certain time without an alarm clock, programming themselves to achieve personal goals and so on. Each is accompanied by a great deal of visualization and imagination which seems to be a very effective way to program the mind and awaken its ESP capabilities.

At the end of the course students are taught to imagine that they are inside physical objects like the walls of their house, a tree leaf, various fruits—visualizing these imaginary scenes as really happening, imagining that the objects are very big or that they are very small so that they can fit easily inside the thing imagined. Finally, they are told to imagine entering the body of a pet and that of a healthy living person they know, seeing all the internal organs and how they are positioned in the body. As the students say, all of these viewings are "just the imagination," but it's remarkable how vivid and detailed these imaginings can be, and in many cases, how accurate.

At the end of this next-to-last class they are told to go home, select three people that they personally know who are sick or disabled, write their names, locations, and ages on separate pieces of paper and bring them in the next day. On this last day each student is told to select a partner they didn't know before they met them in the course. While one takes the role of *psychic* and goes into meditation with their eyes closed, the other whom we'll call the *presenter*, reads only the name, age, and location of one of his or her sick friends. The meditating psychic then tries to identify the subject's illness and give a description of the subject's physical appearance even though the student psychic never met them. All presenters are admonished not to give any hint of their subject's medical condition or physical characteristics when they are acting as presenters.

When the student psychics finally start to work cases of remote people who are ill, they are encouraged to make something up—just imagine what a 25-year-old woman called "Cynthia" in Phoenix would look like if it was up to them to create a character by that name. It doesn't make any difference whether they think they're "right" or not, for them that's Cynthia. It's fantasy time, and if the student psychic approaches the task as he or she did as a child would when playing "let's pretend," the results can be astonishing. Not only do they spot the illness eight or nine times out of ten, but many times they also give an accurate description of the target subject's physical appearance and personality.

The Success of the Silva Method to See People at a Distance

One of the important conditions of the Silva program is that it has a money-back guarantee. If any student feels that the technique didn't work or wasn't worth the time and effort, the instructor must give them their money back. This of course was offered so that potential students would feel confident that they wouldn't be throwing their hard earned cash away. But it also had the effect of encouraging them to avoid giving their psychic partners any hints during the final psychic viewing on the last day. After all, if the remote case-working didn't work, the course was free. As I said in the Preface, this persuaded me to take the course and eventually teach it myself.

Out of the millions who have taken the course around the world, less than 10% have ever asked for their money back. I became aware of this remarkable fact personally because in the three years that I taught Silva, less than 5% asked for their money back, and of course I always gave it to them. But the success stories of the remaining 95% were legion.

In one case, a woman (we'll call her *Hazel*) who was actually unsuccessful herself when she tried to visualize a subject, came to me and said that when she used her father as a case, two different meditating students each said that his hand was damaged. As far as Hazel knew, the only thing that was medically significant about her father was that he had had heart bypass surgery. Since two students had mentioned the same thing, I suggested that she phone her father during the break to check on him. When she came back, obviously emotionally shaken, she said that her father had slammed the car door on his hand just that morning.

One of the reasons why I find this particular event so special among the hundreds of success stories I witnessed is that Hazel was not personally aware of her father's injury. That means there was no way that she could give subtle hints to the meditators about his physical condition. It also means that this was evidence of true clairvoyance and not just mental telepathy, although the latter may indeed be involved in homing in on the case subject. Furthermore, the class was being given in Florida while her father lived in Ohio, and prior to the course Hazel had known neither of the student psychics she used nor they her.

Even if Hazel had tried to remotely view her father's condition herself, she wouldn't have been able to since, as we said above, Hazel was one of the few who were unsuccessful in using their ESP abilities. The reason became clear when Hazel confessed to me that she was a "recreational" user of cocaine.[5] I had already taught two other unsuccessful students in other classes who told me they were drug users (one on barbiturates/amphetamines and the other on Valium). Interestingly enough the ones I taught whom I suspected were alcoholics or at least heavy drinkers were highly successful. Why ESP seemed to work for the alcoholics and not the drug users I encountered I have no idea, but even though the sample was insignificant, it is interesting that hard-drug use and lack of success was so directly correlated in these three cases.

The Failure to Apply the Silva Method to Remote Viewing

You may wonder why I speak of Silva's practical failure when I've just been telling about its extremely high rate of success at teaching people to use their inherent ESP. The failure is not in the method, itself, but in the apparent lack of use by those who have successfully demonstrated that they have psychic ability. People are initially stunned at their success in seeing people at a distance whom they never knew and in describing their illnesses and even their physical appearance. Yet although many still use the techniques they learned in the course, most stop using their case-working ESP faculties completely after a few months or years and seem to forget all about them. Graduates are always welcome to take the course again for nothing, but time and again I've seen many come back who confessed that they never did anything more with psychically viewing remote cases. Why did they eventually ignore this remarkable new ability of theirs? I think there are four major reasons for it:

First this materialistic world of ours is centered on the physical senses, not the extra-sensory. Once graduates have seen the embarrassed disbelief on the faces of friends after describing their psychic experiences to them, few are willing to mention them to anyone else, and most of them gradually stop using the faculty all together. Besides, although they were successful once, why risk failure by trying it again. After all, there is no way that they can kid themselves about their success when the results can be so easily checked against the facts.

Secondly, it's actually easier to simply pick up a phone and call someone than to rely on the sometimes uncertain results of attempted clairvoyance. And when it comes to illnesses, modern medical diagnostic techniques are highly successful. Who needs ESP when a CAT scan, an

---

[5] This was the early 1980's before cocaine was declared illegal. It was still regarded as only mildly addictive and safe to use for recreational purposes.

MRI, or an EKG can show a doctor exactly what the cause of an illness is and where it's located?

Which brings us to the third reason. Before they go into their meditative state for the purpose of viewing remote subjects, students are taught to create an imaginary laboratory in their minds which is filled with tools and medicines they can use to imagine curing the illnesses they encounter. These curing devices can be anything their minds can conjure up, whether they are fantastic, futuristic instruments or ancient, Medieval charms. They are also assisted by two imaginary counselors, one male and one female, whom they assume will have the ability to assist them in curing people and solving problems.

With all these imaginary mental tools and assistants students are encouraged to attempt to heal the people they have detected—and therein lies a problem. Many report success since some people get well or their pain stops. But there is no way, as there is with the descriptions of the illnesses themselves, of proving that what they did with their minds was effective or even a factor in the cure. The students are not stupid. They are as aware of this as anybody else, and after a few "failures," they tend to drift away from the practice even though they may have had what seemed like numerous successes. If the purpose of identifying the illnesses of distant people is to cure them, once that's put into question, there seems to be no good reason to continue the practice.

The fourth reason for Silva's lack of success in persuading students to use their newfound RV abilities is that the course is a commercial one which is sold as a self-help program. Since the majority of students take the course to improve themselves and their lives in the material world, they let this part of the course slide after a while, even though they may feel very good indeed when it seems as if they had actually helped someone get better. But then they get the cases who don't get better, so they forget RV and concentrate on their own problems.

Therefore, for most people it's really not surprising that they don't continue using their case-working abilities. And when you add the materialistic nature of our society, the embarrassment in seeing the disbelief in the eyes of friends and family, and the ease with which many problems can be solved with modern conveniences, there really are few good reasons to continue the practice

But there has recently been a great deal of interest in a phenomenon which may give everyone an excellent reason to look more deeply into the Silva Method as a means to improve their transcendent natures.

The People who Died and Came Back

What has come to be known as Near Death Experiences (NDE) have been reported by hundreds of people and described in a number of recent books, especially one of the first by Raymond A. Moody, Jr., M.D. called *Life After Life*. Some people who have been clinically dead and then revived have spoken of rising out of their bodies, hearing a strange buzzing sound, passing through a dark tunnel with the aid of long lost relatives and friends, seeing an incredibly brilliant light emanating from a loving Being, and going through a life review with Him before being persuaded or deciding to return to the living.

Moody puts the experiences of the 150 subjects in his first book into three categories:

> The experiences of persons who were resuscitated after having been thought, adjudged, or pronounced clinically dead by their doctors.
>
> The experiences of persons who, in the course of accidents or severe injury or illness, came very close to physical death.
>
> The experiences of persons who, as they died, told them to other people who were present. Later, these other people reported the content of the death experience to me [Moody].[6]

As I recounted in the Preface, I had an NDE when I was a child during a minor operation. Since no one ever said that I had died on the operating table, I can only speculate that I may have been one of the ones who "came very close to physical death." But exactly where that dividing line between death and life is supposed to be, nobody really knows. As Moody points out, it's a subject that is hotly debated to this day. In the past it was defined as the point when all detectable bodily functions ceased, usually indicated by no heart beat or breath. Today that's no longer definitive and many say that it's when an EEG shows no sign of brainwaves, when the patient has "flat-lined." Still others claim that it should be defined as the point at which there is no chance of resuscitation. Under the last definition, of course, no one could claim that any person died when they experienced an NDE, but it's much too simplistic and self-defining, and it doesn't really explain how some people could have flat-lined and still come back.

It's interesting that while these experiences are also described in such ancient documents as *The Tibetan Book of the Dead* and Plato's *Republic* (Book X), there is almost no significant record of them up until the 1970's. The reason is that only after modern medical techniques had been devised was it possible to revive some people who had lost all detectable bodily functions. And although many of those techniques were available in the early 20th century, it took another 60 or 70 years for the experiences to be compared and taken seriously.

---

[6] Moody, Raymond A, Jr., M.D.; *Life After Life*; HarperCollins Publishers, Inc., New York; 1975, 2001, p. 8.

Now the question becomes who is this Being of light that everyone seems to meet during an NDE. According to Moody, each person identifies the Being according to their religious beliefs, or lack of belief, at the time of their near death. As Moody reports,

> Interestingly, while the…description of the being of light is utterly invariable, the identification of the being varies from individual to individual and seems to be largely a function of the religious background, training, or beliefs of the person involved.[7]

Thus, Christians have identify him as the Christ, Jews as an angel or God, Buddhists as the Buddha, and atheists as just a "being." In addition, people who have encountered the Being say that conversation with Him is instantaneous and doesn't involve talking, it's strictly mind to mind. Therefore, when they come back they have a difficult time expressing exactly what was said. In addition, the review is utterly unlike anything that they have experienced in the physical world. Some have said it's not really a sequential review of their lives but a four-dimensional instantaneous impression of everything all at once. At the same time they see everything in minute detail and with total participation on their part. The reason for this is probably best described by one woman who said:

> Now, there is a real problem for me as I'm trying to tell you this, because all the words I know are three-dimensional. As I was going through this, I kept thinking, "Well, when I was taking geometry, they always told me there were only three dimensions, and I always just accepted that. But they were wrong. There are more." And, of course, our world—the one we're living in now—is three-dimensional, but the next one definitely isn't. And that's why it's so hard to tell you this. I have to describe it to you in words that are three-dimensional. That's as close as I can get to it, but it's not really adequate.[8]

This astute observation by this woman fits in perfectly with our description of multiple dimensions given in Chapter 2 and explains why so many report that the life review could be comprehended *in toto*. That's exactly the way someone who was transcendent would see our space-time continuum.

The Aftereffects of the NDE

We said above that there seemed to be little if any permanent growth from the spiritual experimentation of the 60's and 70's. But when we come to those who have experienced an NDE, the almost universal effect has been a profound change in their personalities. This is most evident in those who were indifferent or hostile to others. Once they have

---

[7] *Ibid*, p.50.
[8] *Ibid*, pp. 15, 16

gone through a near-death experience, especially the life review, their attitude towards their fellow humans takes a 180 degree turn.

In the life review, NDE's [9] seem not only to see a complete review of their lives but also to experience the effect of their actions towards others. This is not experienced in the context of judgment or condemnation but in the forgiving embrace of that loving Being. It seems that the small acts of kindness we exhibit to others are much more important than our material successes. In a like manner, the snubs and acts of cruelty or indifference which are keenly felt by our acquaintances are felt by us when we experience the review. The joy experienced for their loving acts and the pain of the thoughtless ones is profound and inspires those who have experienced it to completely change their attitude towards others in the years that are left to them in this life.

Moody recounts the story of a man, whom he called Nick, which typifies this reaction in a very dramatic way:

> He was a con artist and an outright criminal who had done everything from bilking widows to running drugs. Crime had provided a good life for Nick. He had nice cars, fine clothes, and new houses, and no problems with his conscience to annoy him.

After he was struck by lightening on a golf course, he experienced an NDE, went through a life review with a being he hesitantly called "God," and...

> ...relived his entire life, not only seeing his actions in three dimensions, but seeing and feeling the effects of his actions on others. That experience changed Nick. Later, while recovering in the hospital, he felt the full effect of his life review. With the being of light, he had been exposed to pure love. He felt that when he really died, he would have to undergo the life review again, a process that would be very uncomfortable if he failed to learn from his first life review. [10]

Needless to say, Nick's life changed completely after this experience, and he is now employed in an "honest and helpful profession."

This experience typifies those of most NDE's. People who were obsessed with money and position switch their priorities completely. They become kinder and place a greater emphasis on loving human relationships. As one woman said about her NDE;

> In life, you can play around and make excuses for yourself and even cover up, and you can stay miserable, if you want to, by doing all this covering up. But when I was there in that review

---

[9] Throughout this book I will use the term "NDE's" to refer to those who have had a near-death experience as well as to the experience, itself. I find the use of the term NDEer's used by many authors much too awkward and contrived.

[10] Moody, Raymond A., M.D.; *The Light Beyond: New Explorations by the Author of Life after Life*; Bantam Books, New York, paperback edition, 1988, pp. 35,36.

there was no covering up. I was the very people that I hurt, and I was the very people I helped to feel good. I wish I could find some way to convey to everyone how good it feels to know that you are responsible and to go through something like this where it is impossible not to face it.[11]

Obviously, this woman was delighted to find out that her freedom to choose her path through life was real. She really was in control of many things in her life that she previously blamed on "fate" or the actions of others.

While many NDE's may not relish their responsibility in the same way that this woman does, they all agree that the message is the same—it is essential to our own well being to "Do unto others as you would have them do unto you." We will, by God, be kind and loving with one another or face the consequences—not the consequences of hell-fire, but those that are self inflicted in the presence of a loving Being who is giving us a perfect example of what love really is. Can you imagine what it would be like to be an Adolf Hitler or a Joseph Stalin and experience the pain and death they caused to millions upon millions of people, *en mass*?

While it isn't surprising that NDE's no longer fear death after their experience on the "other side," it is surprising that most seem to have little desire to end this life to return to that spiritual paradise. In fact, they usually experience a higher feeling of urgency to correct the problems of this world and to deal with them with love and understanding. Knowledge is essential for change, and they have a strong desire to attain that knowledge. In fact, they come away from their experience with the conviction that the two most important things in life are love and knowledge.

The feelings of universality, of connectedness with all things, is not untypical of all kinds of meditation and mystical experiences, and usually leads to a more spiritual life. Interestingly, most NDE's find the distinctions between religions to be unimportant—theology seems to hold little interest although spirituality is extremely important to them and occupies a great deal of their thoughts and actions. Therefore, while some of them who come from more traditional religious backgrounds may stay in those institutions, they express little interest in orthodox religious dogma and dismiss it as unimportant. They stay because they're more apt to find their kind of spiritual awareness in other members in these institutions than in more secular environments, and through prayer and meditations can reconnect with that wonderful transcendent world they experienced.

As for me, it's hard for me to remember any specific changes that might have taken place after I had my NDE except for one thing. Before my NDE, I had followed my mother's advice to pray to Jesus whenever I was scared because he would always be there to comfort me. Although I still thought of myself as a Christian, as a child I never again asked Jesus for

---

[11] *Ibid*, p. 47.

comfort or protection after the operation. At the time I found it very puzzling, but I just could not bring myself to do it. As we said above, the identification of the Being for most people is a function of their religious background, but I guess that wasn't the case for me. Although I'm very vague about this, my impression is that I simply assumed I'd had a conversation with God, Himself, in my NDE and therefore directed my prayers to Him.

In addition, I can only assume that the experience might have been an additional motivation for me to pursue a career in religion as well as science.

A Word of Caution

The thing which makes the accounts of the original NDE's so compelling is the almost identical nature of their experiences before there had been any publicity about them. Since the publication of Moody's book and other general NDE books, a large number have been published by individuals describing their own experiences which are considerably longer and more complex. I have not found any of the latter which agree with one another. Without this agreement the single way we have of assuming the authenticity of these experiences is lost, and we can only say that although they may seem real for the people who report them, the rest of us must view them with a great deal of skepticism. It is far too tempting for people to want to stand out in a crowd and draw attention to themselves by saying in effect, "Yeah, those NDE's are OK, but wait till you hear what happened to *me!*" And if you're going to write a saleable book, two pages describing a typical NDE isn't going to hack it.

It's also typical of humans to want to protect reality schemes in which they have invested a great deal of their faith and loyalty. For instance, one such account sounded like it came straight from a Roman Catholic catechism with conversations with the Virgin Mary and messages that would gladden the heart of any Catholic priest. Another sounds like a handbook for mediums and still another talks of a group of spiritual councilors giving detailed instructions for building enlightenment rooms. None of these longer accounts can be taken at face value, and indeed their proliferation detracts from the essential message of the core experience. The original simple accounts given to researchers like Moody and Kenneth Ring, especially the ones recounted by children who presumably had no axe to grind, are the ones that should be given the greatest credence. They may attribute the identity of the Being of light to their own particular religious deity, but there is little if any variation in their descriptions of the Being's nature. And their message is always the same and isn't very much different from the one which a woman in one of Andrew Greeley's books experiences when she senses something called the "Presence."

...There was no forgiveness, no blame, no lifting of burdens of guilt, no message that at last she was forgiven. Rather, the love that surrounded Nora behaved as though it had never left, chided her gently for not noticing its presence, and enveloped her in caressing and tender warmth. Embraced by such love, Nora realized how irrelevant was forgiveness, how foolish was anger, and how ridiculous was guilt.[12]

The Connection Between the NDE and ESP

I said above that all the major religions of the world except for Hinduism were a *sample of one*. But as Moody says, "Pollster George Gallup, Jr., found that eight million adults in the United States have had an NDE. That equals one person in twenty."[13] That's a pretty impressive data base, much more so than the ones on which we have based our major religions.

What these experiences indicate is that there is a transcendent spiritual world that exists in parallel with our material one. As I said above, over the millennia we have attempted to contact that world through prayer, meditation, trance, and the incantations and intercessions of shamans and priests. The results have been spotty at best.

What would happen if we could duplicate the experience of the NDE without nearly dying? There have been cases of people duplicating parts of the experience under stressful conditions. Moody recounts the experience of a sergeant in Sicily in World War II. When his platoon was pinned down by a German machine-gun crew, he circled around them and threw a grenade into their nest that didn't go off. They immediately turned their gun on him, and while he lay curled up waiting to be hit, he "left" his body in an out-of-body experience. As he recounted it to Moody:

> As I lay there, I suddenly left my body, and Sicily for that matter. I "traveled" to a munitions plant in New Jersey, where I floated over an assembly line of women who were putting hand grenades together. I tried to talk to them and tell them to pay attention to their work, but they wouldn't listen. Instead they kept chattering as they did their work.[14]

He goes on to say that after what seemed like fifteen or twenty minutes, he suddenly "returned" to Sicily, threw another grenade into the nest which exploded, killing the Germans, and then he calmly returned to his platoon. He was so calm that they figured something was mentally wrong with him

---

[12] Greeley, Andrew M.; *Thy Brother's Wife*; Warner Books, Inc., New York, N.Y., 1983, p. 398. From this, one would think that Greeley had had an NDE of his own—and perhaps in a way he did.

[13] *Moody*, p. 6.

[14] *Ibid*, p. 97.

and sent him to a psychiatrist. After he told his story, the psychiatrist's response was rather unusual:

> He told me that he had heard of this happening to other men before, and that I should keep the experience to myself so I wouldn't get sent to him again. That's exactly what I did.

Since this seems not to be an uncommon experience for soldiers in combat, it indicates, just like the Silva Method does, that we don't have to die to experience transcendence.

If what the sergeant and the other combat soldiers experienced was a real out-of-body event, then they participated in something that many NDE's go through. Very often they find themselves floating above their bodies, watching the medical personnel working on them. Sometimes they even find themselves drifting to the waiting room and can describe what their relatives and friends are wearing and talking about. In one case Moody recounts the experience of an NDE who saw during his out-of-body experience (OBE) that one of his relatives had put on miss-matched socks in his haste to get to the hospital, a fact that was later confirmed. It is the accuracy of these events that many point to as reliable evidence that what they experienced was real and not just something their minds made up.

Kenneth Ring in his book, *Lessons from the Light,* tells of an even more compelling example of an OBE by a woman, a migrant worker called Maria, who had a severe heart attack. As reported by her social worker, Kimberly Clark, Maria said she rose out of her body and eventually found herself outside the building on the third floor of the north wing of the hospital. Kimberley wasn't about to believe such a fanciful tale until Maria reported spotting something in her OBE that was so bizarre that she had to check it out. Maria said she saw, of all things, a tennis shoe on the ledge of the building and that "the little toe had a worn place in the shoe and…one of its laces was tucked underneath the heel." Clark went to the third floor and when she looked out the middle window, there was the tennis shoe precisely as Maria had described it. Ring[15] goes on to say that it's hard to imagine how anyone could claim that Maria was hallucinating when she could hardly have known about the shoe on a ledge above her physical location in a hospital in a large city she was visiting for the first time as a migrant worker. Of course if a skeptic were to admit that such an experience couldn't be a hallucination, he would have to give up his firmly held belief that the mind and body were inseparable. And of course that would mean that there was a whole other spiritual realm that we might very well be able to experience.

---

[15] Ring, Kenneth, Ph.D.; *Lessons from the Light—What we can learn from the near-death experience*; Moment Point Press, Portsmith, N.H., 1998, p. 66.

Can We Artificially Induce an NDE?

We have seen that adults who go through an NDE tend to change dramatically. Let's suppose that we can give the NDE experience to anyone without nearly killing them. What kind of technique could we use to train them to contact that wonderful transcendent world and change their lives and subsequently the lives of the people around them? If it could be done, it might be the catalyst that would finally point this poor old beat-up world of ours in the right direction—the direction the flower children of the 60's and 70's were striving so hard to reach.

In his book, *Lessons from the Light*, Kenneth Ring implies that something like this can be accomplished simply by vicariously absorbing the experiences of the NDE's. He has a point. It is indeed inspirational to read about these experiences and what they did for the people who had them. But no one would argue with the fact that it isn't the same as actually experiencing the event, itself.

Countless other books have claimed that they can teach you to hypnotize yourself into experiencing transcendence or meditating to achieve enlightenment. Few who have attempted these techniques progress beyond accomplishing a "feel-good" state or perhaps an increased ability to handle stress, and few if any can point to specific evidence that they accomplished anything other than these admirable but simple goals. Many of those who practice yoga can assume the Lotus position, intone their mantras with impressive breath control, and contort their bodies into the many yoga exercise positions, but none in my experience have ever achieved the enlightenment claimed by the famous gurus. In fact among the supposed "experts" in Yoga who took my Silva class very few were able to see the distant-viewing cases presented to them or describe their illnesses, while the housewives, truckers, business men, bikers, and school children around them did so with ease. It made me think that maybe at least some of the apparent success of these Eastern techniques was more the product of self-deception rather than spiritual enlightenment.

That leads me to suggest that no technique has much chance of simulating an NDE unless it can demonstrate success in performing transcendental feats that can be verified. Silva and the more recent CIA-devised, remote-viewing courses are such techniques but they are at the very beginning of a fledgling endeavor. It might behoove us to take these techniques or something very much like them and see if we can deepen the experience to the point where we can actually contact that marvelous transcendent world and perhaps even the Being of light as well.

As we said above, the failure of the Silva graduates to use the case-working portion of the course after graduating is not the fault of the technique but of the focus of the course. If we contact the graduates who have been very successful at case working or remote viewing and take them through a spiritually modified version, one that is focused on the events experienced by the NDE's, then perhaps we can cross the barrier that separates us from the transcendent. No one has ever tried this before so one can only speculate what would happen, but it holds a promise for a future that could be awe inspiring.

This is not an endeavor that should be undertaken lightly. The worst that could probably happen is nothing since as far as we know no one in our modern society has ever brought about their own death by mere thought. However, if it is possible to contact this transcendent world, it could result in a personal transformation of unprecedented intensity. No one can know for sure one way or the other until it's tried.

However, I suspect that when we do, we will experience something that is so extraordinary that we will never be the same again. Life as we know it will change, because once we have experienced the world beyond this one, all that we thought was once so important will be insignificant. But while we may lose the exciting busy-busy life we were so entangled with, we will gain a vision of our own potential that will surpass our wildest dreams. We have said that our spirit is not trapped by the natural forces of our material world, but can change itself and become the most powerful and transcendent force in the universe. We are the reason that miracles can happen; we don't need to grovel in obeisance before a vengeful god we have created in our own imagination with our misguided feelings of guilt. Faith in arbitrary commandments by ego-driven gurus, shamans, ministers, and priests can be replaced with the direct knowledge of what that transcendent world is really like.

Chapter 7

What's It All About?

If humanity is really transcendent, then the universe must be some kind of medium for the development and advancement of our spiritual natures. Instead of being a testing ground so that God can find out who's been naughty or nice, it's just as Origen speculated: *this* is the place where we are meant to be in order to develop into the beings we must become. I suspect that there is no permanent escape from it into heaven or nirvana until we have achieved that ultimate destiny. I also suspect that we must return to it time and time again, to learn and develop from it, not because we have been bad and must be punished until we turn our karma into a bright shiny new penny, but because we have a higher purpose that we must attain.

Take for instance the experience of the NDE's. The life review was a check on how well they did during their lifetimes in relating to their fellow humans. Why? It seems that we are supposed to increase the most important part of our connection—a connection which we call love—that we have not only with our human brothers and sisters but also with all life forms. That in turn would imply that Teilhard is right, that there is a new sphere being developed, whether you call it Omega or Beta, that is going to result in something like a new world-wide spiritual sphere.

Which brings up the second half of this equation. We are here not only to develop our transcendent natures, but to improve our lives and the lives of everyone around us. More and more doctors, psychiatrists, and scientists have come to realize that what we think of ourselves is what we become. Time and time again doctors have seen spontaneous cures when patients practice meditation, pray, use biofeedback techniques, or even invoke laughter to fight their diseases. Psychiatrists have witnessed the damage that past commands that have lodged in the subconscious have done to all of us. By repeating them endlessly to ourselves, we become the very type of person we don't want to be. And even science in the form of quantum mechanics has shown scientists that the observer plays an intimate part in the examination of nature and have made many realize that thought, itself, must influence the very cells of the body and perhaps even their fate in the external world.

We are actually in charge. We can not only change ourselves, but it seems that we can change our fate as well. The woman mentioned in Chapter 6 who was delighted when she learned in her NDE that she was responsible for everything that she did was not only talking about her own actions, but about her so-called fate in life. She knew that she could actually influence it in a profound way. If that's true for all of us, what would happen if we all had this ability and used it? Would we all merge into one amorphous *Gaia* mass, losing our identities in the process?

Frankly, I don't think so. Along with Teilhard's complexification of life, there has also been a complexification of individuality. No one would expect a drone bee to do anything other than what all the other drone bees do. But as you ascend the life-complexification ladder, individuality becomes more and more apparent until you come to humanity where the best and brightest become quite unique. One would be hard pressed to find an equivalent Mozart, Einstein, Shakespeare, or Gandhi. That would seem to suggest that as we progress spiritually, our individuality will become more pronounced, not less.

The truth of the matter is that we don't know what comes next. What I suggest that we do know is that according to the NDE's our primary goal in this world is a compassionate concern for our fellow humans and a desire to acquire as much information about our lives and our universe as possible.

And after acquiring that information, we may find that the universe, itself, can point us in the right direction.

The Structured Universe

We are surrounded by the fruits of the science that dominates our society. But while we may realize that all our material benefits—the cars, TV sets, cell phones, etc.—are the direct result of the discoveries of science, we seldom appreciate the fact that science has proven that our material world is logically structured. Before science revealed the logical consistency of the laws of nature, no one could be sure that their lives weren't directed by the whims of the gods or the vagaries of magical forces. In fact, the archeological Stonehenges of the past are most likely the engines of manipulation with which ancient man hoped to gain some control over those whimsical deities or at least predict their designs. But now we can be assured that the material effects that govern our lives are the result of logically consistent natural causes, even though many people may still cling to the perhaps more comfortable superstitions of the past. The universe is indeed logically structured.

When I was studying computer programming, one of the computer languages we learned was called *Pascal*, a highly structured language designed to teach students how to produce code that could be easily understood by any other programmer who had to fix our computer programs. While studying this language, I came across the following ditty:

> Pascal is a structured language,
> It's as structured as can be.
> It structures all my programs,
> And now it's structuring me.

It was not only amusing, it was also remarkably true. Many of us realized that we were starting to think in a more logically consistent way, not only with our programs but in our lives as well.

The truth is that the material universe is doing something like that but not exactly in the same way. You might say that the logical nature of the material world *encourages* sentient beings to think logically, but it certainly doesn't guarantee it.

An individual gazelle or wildebeest might not have the reasoning powers to conclude that it wouldn't be wise to graze next to a pride of lions even though they were sleeping off a meal, but natural selection would eventually assure that the majority would keep their distance. So we could say that gradual evolution tends to eliminate what we would call "illogical" behavior among species, leaving only those who conform to the "logical" laws of nature.

Now let's consider major ecological changes—massive meteor strikes, ice ages, volcanic activity, and continental plate shifts causing mountain ranges and rift valleys all have been cited as causes of massive extinctions over millions of years. These are rare, but when they occur, whole species can change or be eliminated. It's almost as if nature were saying that even successful adaptation is only temporary. Every hundred million years or so life's going to have to change. And indeed it has, time and time again.

That is, it did until evolution produced us.

Suddenly—you might say almost instantaneously as far as geological time is concerned—we have come on the scene and can actually avoid these catastrophes before they happen. As reasoning animals we can cultivate our own food, house ourselves, prevent diseases, medically repair ourselves, and predict the coming of disasters with greater and greater accuracy. And we are the only ones who have ever had this capability in the approximately four billion years that life has been on this planet.

So now instead of evolution changing us, we can change evolution! We now have the power, through the intelligence that evolution has bestowed on us, to change not only our environment but ourselves as well. It's as if nature's periodic cycle of species' death and new species' birth were putting life on different paths, time after time, until it finally produced a rational species which could break the cycle.

The Possibility of a Moral Universe

Since science has proved that logical reasoning works remarkably well in the universe, then applying that logical reasoning to morals should be just as successful. Consider for example some of our more common sayings: "cheat me once, shame on you—cheat me twice, shame on me;" "never trust someone who says, 'I give you my word'," nor anyone who "protests too much;" and of course there's the perennial "don't cry over spilt milk." These are truisms that we have learned through practical trial and error in a universe in which survival is awarded to those who are best adapted to its environment. In these cases, survival is not a life-or-death issue, but a quality-of-life issue. Thus, we might be living in a 13.7-billion-year-old universe that encourages what we could call *moral* behavior. That is, we could if these practical admonitions were considered to be moral in the sense of "the best for everyone," and not "because God said so."

For example, take Jesus's admonition to "turn the other cheek." Everyone seems to claim that that's the epitome of saintly moral behavior and nobody really believes it. Evolution has given every animal, including us, what is called the "fight or flight" syndrome. If you think you can win, then fight the good fight—if not, then run away. Anyone who is in a conflict situation where they feel they can do neither are candidates for the psychiatrist's couch or the ovens at Dachau. Israel has learned that lesson extremely well.

While few really believe that you should turn the other cheek in a fist fight, even fewer believe that the meek will really inherit the Earth if there are monsters like Adolph Hitler, Joseph Stalin, Saddam Hussein, or Genghis Khan around—or that it would be possible to love a neighbor as yourself if he raped and killed your wife and daughters while you watched.

These admonitions by Jesus might make sense and might be easily achieved if you think the end of the world is going to come in a few weeks or months. But the moral universe says that if you're planning to live a long and useful life, some of these admonitions are going to deny you that worthy goal *and you'd better realize that before proceeding and accepting the consequences*.

For example, some people have pointed to Gandhi as a practical example of the efficacy of passive resistance. However, when they do, they're ignoring the fact that Gandhi was protesting against a British Empire which made "fair play" and "acting like a gentlemen" virtually a national fetish. He wouldn't have lasted three weeks in Nazi Germany.

Which brings us to a very important aspect of moral behavior— effective morality depends on the circumstances. For example, an ethics professor of mine in seminary asked our class of aspiring future priests what a Christian nation should do if it had a grain surplus and a Third-World nation was starving. Naturally, we all said that the well-off Christians should supply the starving natives with all the grain they needed.

"Excellent," proclaimed the professor, "you have just demonstrated your Christian charity while condemning an entire nation to a life-time of poverty! The sole source of income for the poor nation was the production and sale of grain. By providing them with an unlimited supply of free grain, you have destroyed their economy."

So here we have a dilemma. We can't just go blundering along mindlessly applying these compassionate laws without analyzing the consequences. In some cases, like the problem the professor posed, the solution is relatively obvious and can again be found in a common saying: "Feed a man a fish and you feed him for a day—teach him how to fish and you feed him for a life-time." But remember, practical experience in a logical universe taught us that, not some commandment handed down from above. Even the Ten Commandments were derived for practical reasons in a practical universe that I'm sure Moses was very expert at interpreting.

However, there are some cases where the course to follow isn't obvious. Fortunately, there's a relatively new technique that has been developed over the last century which can help us in our decision making.

Game Theory

Game theory is an outgrowth of the kind of calculations that were and still are being used to determine the odds in games of chance. These same calculations were eventually applied to more complex human, social, military, and economic applications and came to be known as game theory. In its present stage of development, game theory is quite primitive and depends on rather simple arbitrary conditions of rewards and penalties, but it has led to some very interesting conclusions. For example, in a competition to decide which strategy would be the most successful in resolving conflicts between two individual entities, the strategy called "Tit for Tat" easily won. Its simple design was that if an adversary attacked you, you must respond immediately with an attack of your own. If he backs off, then you back off. Tit for Tat.

However, latter refinement of the game showed that as it progressed over a period of time, it was not as successful as originally thought since an aggressor who cleverly modified his strategy would eventually come out on top and upset the equilibrium. But that's the point. The universe doesn't guarantee success in such a confrontation, but only if both sides have developed to the point where winning just for the sake of winning is no longer considered to be a logical goal. We must use our societal intelligence to assure that all members of society have achieved that enlightenment.

However, the unsophisticated nature of strategies such as this is uncovered when one examines the history of conflicts such as the recent ones in WWII, Korea, Vietnam, Iraq, and Israel. Human conflicts are much more complex than the simple scenarios of current game theory. However, it is the first step in a fledgling discipline that promises to evolve over time into a truly effective "moral" strategy, one that is dictated by nature and not handed down to us from any self-proclaimed prophet of God.

However, since it is implicit that these possible solutions to human conflicts are imbedded in the very nature of this apparently deliberately-created universe, it seems logical to conclude they are what the creator intended for us to discover, using our intelligence and free will. But if that's true, then the universe has been structured to produce not only intelligent life but a particular kind of intelligent life that leads to stability and harmony sometime and somewhere in its vastness.

Now for the Big Question: Why?

It's the one seemingly unanswerable question that humanity has been asking itself for millennia. Why are we here? What's the purpose of our existence? And of course it's the one question that science, our most potent tool for answering questions, is incapable of answering. To materialists it's a question that shouldn't be asked in the first place because it's meaningless. We're here because we're here.

When the universe was thought to be infinite and eternal, that was a non-answer that was hard to ignore. We are apparently the result of natural forces, so why keep asking such questions and not just make the best of it?

But now science, itself, has discovered that the universe had a beginning and presumably has an end. Once we realized that it was apparently designed very precisely to support life and may even encourage intelligent life, and when we discovered that matter was more like amorphous waves of energy governed by probabilities rather than certainties, the "why" question took on a new validity. It has not only become a legitimate question to ask, it has become imperative to seek the answer.

Let's face it—we really can kill ourselves. We can stop the whole procedure from continuing on Earth, and now that we have that power, we'd better find out what we should do with it to fulfill whatever destiny the Maker of the universe had in mind.

Unfortunately, I don't think our current religions can supply the answer. As we've said, they're based on cosmologies that put us on a kind of center stage that makes the religious supposition that this is a kind of moral testing ground with rewards and punishments at the end of our lives a viable concept. But when you consider the gradual evolution of the universe into a more and more complex physical entity and the accompanying evolution of life forms from single cells to mega-molecular animals, the testing theory no longer makes any sense.

But if this isn't a testing ground to determine who's been "good" and who's been "bad," what in the world is the universe designed for and why are we here? The gradual development of matter and life into more and more complex entities must be part of it.

That's why I think that the purpose of this universe is to change us into a different kind of being. According to Teilhard, we are destined to become like Jesus with all his compassion, wisdom, and remarkable healing abilities. Why? I would guess that Teilhard would believe that it was so we could merge with God in a very Hindu-like concept of union with Brahma. But that brings up more questions than it answers.

For example, what kind of transcendental entities were we before we became a part of this transformation machine called the universe? And why would it be so important that we become a part of the entity that supposedly created the machine in the first place? According to my thesis here, we are fifth-dimensional souls that have existed before this universe was created and will continue to do so after it dies. But what were we before life started its evolution in the universe? This is something that we can never hope to know in our lifetimes, but there are definite clues as to what we should become, no matter what we were before.

The NDE's, Jesus of Nazareth, and countless holy men and women of the past have all claimed that love, compassion, and deep concern for our fellow life-forms are our prime directives. If we really believe that, then what religion we believe in doesn't matter a hill of beans because we already know what we should be doing regardless of what the priests, the writers of Bibles, and the countless theological bureaucrats want us to do. So at least one of our goals is to worry less about belief and more about our actions in relation to others.

How to Create Your Own Heaven and Leave Hell to the Misinformed

The NDE's have given us a path to follow that is simple and direct. It amazes me that no one seems to take them seriously when it comes to their experiences of the life review. What they are describing is what heaven and hell are really like. We apparently create both of them. In the loving embrace of that Being of light they experienced with great joy the many seemingly insignificant kind things they did for people and with great pain the thoughtless and mean things. They came to realize that they were the ones who were responsible for their ultimate destiny.

So following the advice of the NDE's, our best bet is to take delight in our fellow human beings, love the life we've got, and give whatever comfort and help we can to others, whether they are less or more fortunate than ourselves. Pretty straight-forward stuff, but apparently one of life's prime directives.

But don't forget the second imperative mentioned by the NDE's— the pursuit of knowledge. Without it we can make huge mistakes that permit us to ignore our prime directive to love others as ourselves. The most obvious is assigning whole groups of people to the status of inferior races. Blacks become niggers, Jews become kikes, Italians become wops, Chinese become gooks—the list goes on and on, and it gives the unthinking the implied impression that they can do anything to them that they want, resulting in slavery, ghettos, and the wholesale slaughter of innocents.

And of course we shouldn't forget our totally insane practice of killing anyone who doesn't believe as we do, thereby making sure that they'll never have the opportunity to correct their "heretical" thinking. That only can be justified if you believe that you are one of the pre-ordained elect who will be "saved," that there is no such thing as free will, and that everyone else is doomed anyway so it's OK to help them achieve their destiny.

But does the action of the universe ensure that this type of thinking will eventually be eradicated? Of course not! Once the evolutionary forces have produced a rational entity, it's up to that entity to reason itself beyond primitive limbic-brain reactions and change its own destiny. If not, the evolved entity itself, like we humans, will unwittingly terminate the experiment and evolution will try again. Remember, the universe has infinite patience.

We must never forget that *we are not the center of the universe.* It's not surprising that we seem to forget that since it was only very recently that we discovered that we weren't. Now it's evident that there must be other "Earths" out there among the billions upon billions of planets. They will experience the same evolutionary forces evident here, so some of them will probably produce the result the universe was designed for.

Dean Koontz described in his book, *Sole Survivor,* what might happen to us if we do achieve that goal. When his hero experiences something very much like an NDE, he describes his revelation in a way that parallels this discussion in a remarkable way:

> He understood that eternal life was not an article of faith but a law of the universe as true as any law of physics. The universe is an efficient creation: matter becomes energy, energy becomes matter; one form of energy is converted into another form; the balance is forever changing, but the universe is a closed system from which no particle of matter or wave of energy is ever lost. Nature not only loathes waste but forbids it. The human mind and spirit, at their noblest, can transform the material world for the better; we can even transform the human condition, lifting ourselves from a state of primal fear, when we dwelled in caves and shuddered at the sight of the moon, to a position from which we can contemplate eternity and hope to understand the works of God. Light cannot change itself into stone by an act of *will,* and stone cannot build itself into temples. Only the human spirit can act with volition and consciously change itself; it is the only thing in all creation that is not entirely at the mercy of forces outside itself; and it is, therefore, the most powerful and valuable form of energy in the universe. For a time, the spirit may become flesh, but when that phase

of its existence is at an end, it will be transformed into a disembodied spirit once more.[1]

With this insightful paragraph Dean Koontz sums up the previous hundred-plus pages of this book in a few short words. It is now up to us to see if this transformation is possible and that the apparent ultimate goal of life in this universe can be achieved here on mother Earth.

---

[1] Koontz, Dean; *Sole Survivor*, Ballantine Books, New York, 1977, p. 402.

Bibliography

Brad Lemley, "Why is There Life?", *Discover* magazine, November, 2000, p.64.

Durant, Will, *The Story of Civilization: Part III, Caesar and Christ*, Simon and Schuster, New York, 1944.

Durant, Will, The Story of Civilization: Part IV, The Age of Faith, Simon and Schuster, New York, 1950.

Elliston, Ron, "Parapsychology in Intelligence: The Rise and Fall of the CIA's Psychic Spies," http://www.parascope.com/ds/articles/CIAparapsychology.htm.

The Five Gospels: The Search for the Authentic Words of Jesus, New Translation and Commentary by Robert W. Funk, Roy W. Hoover, and The Jesus Seminar, Macmillan Publishing Co., New York, 1993.

Fredriksen, Paula, *Jesus of Nazareth, King of the Jews*, Alfred A. Knopf, New York, 1999.

Fredriksen, Paula, *Who He Was*, http://www.tnr.com/101501/frecriksen101501_print.html .

George Berkeley: Principles of Human Knowledge / Three Dialogues, edited by Roger Woolhouse, Penguin Books, New York, NY, 1988.

Greeley, Andrew M., *Thy Brother's Wife*, Warner Books, Inc., New York, N.Y., 1983.

Koontz, Dean, *Sole Survivor*, Ballantine Books, New York, 1977.

Kreisberg, Jennifer Cobb, "A Globe, Clothing Itself with a Brain," *Wired* magazine, Issue 3.06, June, 1995.

Kress, Kenneth A., "Parapsychology in Intelligence: A Personal Review and Conclusions," *Studies in Intelligence*, http://www.parascope.com/ds/articles/parapsychologyDoc.htm.

Moody, Raymond A, Jr., M.D., *Life After Life*, Bantam Books, New York, 1975.

Moody, Raymond A., M.D., *The Light Beyond: New Explorations by the Author of Life after Life*, Bantam Books, New York, paperback edition, 1989.

Nasar, Sylvia, *A Beautiful Mind*, A Touchstone Book Published by Simon & Schuster, New York, 2001.

Pagels, Elaine H., *The Gnostic Gospels*, Vintage Books, A Division of Random House, Inc., New York, 1979.

Penrose, Roger, *The Emperor's New Mind*, Penguin Books, 1991.

Penrose, Roger, *Shadows of the Mind*, Oxford University Press, 1994.

The Philosophical Writings of Descartes, Volumes I-III, translated by John Cottingham, Robert Stoothoff, and Dugald Murdoch, Cambridge University Press, 1984.

Ring, Kenneth, Ph.D., *Lessons from the Light—What we can learn from the near-death experience*, Moment Point Press, Portsmith, N.H., 1998.

Rubenstein, Richard E., *When Jesus Became God*, Harcourt, Inc., New York,1999.

Sagan, Carl, *Cosmos*, Random House, New York, 1980.

Schrödinger, Erwin, Translator: John D. Trimmer, "The Present Situation in Quantum Mechanics," *Proceedings of the American Philosophical Society*, 1935.

Schweitzer, Albert, *The Quest for the Historical Jesus*, Edited by John Bowden, Fortress Press, Minneapolis, 2001.

Smith, Paul H., *Reading the Enemy's Mind: Inside Star Gate—America's Psychic Espionage Program*, A Tom Doherty Associates Book, New York, 2005.

Teilhard de Chardin, *The Phenomenon of Man*, Harper Torchbooks, Harper & Row, New York, translated from the French by Bernard Wall, 1959.

Index

800756

Made in the USA